D1116264

Revolution and Religion

Revolution and Religion

American Revolutionary War and the Reformed Clergy

Keith L. Griffin

PARAGON HOUSE
New York, New York

First edition, 1994

Published in the United States by

Paragon House
370 Lexington Avenue
New York, New York 10017

Library of Congress Cataloging-in-Publication Data
    Revolution and religion : American Revolutionary War and the
Reformed clergy / Keith L. Griffin — 1st ed.
        p.   cm.
    Includes bibliographical references and index.
    ISBN 1-55778-590-2
    1. Middle Atlantic States—Church history—18th century.
    2. Reformed Church—Middle Atlantic States—Clergy. 3. Clergy—
Middle Atlantic States—Political activity. 4. Just war doctrine.
    5. Middle Atlantic States—History—Colonial period, ca. 1600–1775.
    6. Middle Atlantic States—History—Revolution, 1775–1783.
    I. Title.
    BR520.G75   1994
    261.8′73′097409033—dc20   92-38186
                                                                CIP

Manufactured in the United States of America

To Stella,
for all the sacrifices,
and Adrina, Naomi, and Elyse
for waiting.

Contents

1

Sixteenth Century Resistance Ideology

INTRODUCTION

What the ordained middle colony Reformed clergy preached and wrote in support of war against foreign aggressors or revolution against domestic tyrants forms the central subject matter of this monograph. It will examine the conditions under which the middle colony Reformed ministers thought it necessary and sufficient for Christians to take up arms against an oppressor. The middle colony Reformed clergy's arguments for revolution against the British Crown in the eighteenth century can be seen better as an extension of the theological heritage of Reformed Protestantism rather than as an abrupt shift from that tradition's arguments to reliance on contemporary political ideology.

Demonstration of that extension into the thought and preaching of the middle colony Reformed clergy requires an overview of the earlier Reformed resistance statements, for, though Reformed theology varied in the finer points, it remained remarkably consistent throughout the sixteenth, seventeenth, and eighteenth centuries. Within that time span, there arose numerous instances in which Reformed ministers were challenged to respond to the same question of whether or not they and their congregations should resist oppressive rulers, or repel aggressive invaders.

Though the biblical position of obedience to the ruling authorities remained the starting point of the political ethics of Reformed ministers throughout the centuries, Reformed theology in general retained a potential for justifying violent resistance to oppression and aggression. Reformed theologians never condoned offensive war, but their justifications of defensive war

1

consistently returned to much the same tenets. First, the Reformed clergy accepted the validity of a just war. Second, these men inevitably pointed to the natural law of self-defense. Third, they believed that, in the midst of a defensive war, God intervened on behalf of His Covenant people, though his providence worked through the means of his people. Fourth, Reformed preachers often justified defensive war on the basis of the requirements of a national covenant with God.

The political upheavals, in the midst of which Reformed ministers and theologians forged their instruments of ideological warfare, were spread across both Europe and America from 1520 to 1780. Some of those quill-and-ink weapons were also borne by the American middle colony Reformed clergy in the mid-eighteenth century to justify war against the French and revolution against the British; a direct line for an enduring few of those concepts can be drawn from the sixteenth century Reformation to the era of the American Revolution. Thus, after profiling early Reformation pieces dealing with resistance, attention will be given to the writings of the Marian exiles and John Knox. Clearly, the line to the middle colony Reformed ideology of war and revolution can be traced from the sixteenth century Calvinists through the Puritan resistance writers of the seventeenth century in both old and New England, and since Puritan resistance theories constituted the most immediate and greatest influences on the middle colony Reformed clergy's concepts of war and revolution, more attention will be given the Puritans than continental developments.

Although this book traces the Reformed ideology of resistance, it must be remembered that the bedrock foundation of Reformed political ethics continued to be submission to and obedience to the authority of political authorities on the basis of clear Scriptural injunctions. Thus, not only the ideological continuities will be examined, but also the peculiarities of circumstance that jarred Reformed theory from that course of obedience.

SUBMISSION

The Reformation was, from its earliest years, a resistance movement, a movement setting itself against entrenched authorities, born in an era when there was no separation of church from state. Church and state worked conjointly to enforce God's will on society in the Roman version of the *corpus christianum*; thus, Reformed Protestantism developed in response to that system an ideology of armed resistance to political and ecclesiastical oppression, and formulated, as well, its own perspective on the church and its relationship to temporal powers.

However, without doubt, Protestants in the sixteenth century declared the starting point of their political ethic to be that Christians owed to the magistrate obedience.[1] Christians were to obey the magistrate regardless of the latter's personal competence, morality, or religion. To bolster that foundation standard arguments were employed such as: the fact that government *per se* is divinely ordained by God in the Scriptures; bad rulers were sent by God to chastise the nation for their sins;[2] rebellion causes more harm to innocents than to the guilty;[3] and the king is above judgment by the lower classes. A classic statement of the last argument was made by William Tyndale (1494 ? –1536), for example, who wrote:

> God hath made the king in every realm judge over all, and over him there is no judge. He that judgeth the king judgeth God, and he that layeth hand on the king layeth hand on God . . . If the subjects sin, they must be brought to the king's judgement. If the king sin, he must be reserved unto the judgement, wrath and vengeance of God.[4]

Other English theologians in the early Reformation, both Anglo-Catholic and Reformed, such as Stephen Gardiner, Robert Barnes, and Hugh Latimer, held the same sort of opinion about resistance.[5] In this tradition, the king's law *was*, at least in practice, God's law.[6] On the other hand, while Christian thinkers had always set forth the belief in submission as foundational to their political ethics, the Reformation writers had it tested so severely by the oppression brought about by Roman Catholic rulers that at least some qualifications were ineluctable.

In spite of the general obedience principle, all of the sixteenth century Reformers allowed passive disobedience should a ruler command that which was manifestly contrary to biblical laws or injunctions.[7] The disagreement, though, over whether the victims of tyranny may *actively* resist the actions or commands of a tyrant formed one of the major divisions among Protestants in this period. Another major division was created by disagreement about whether the ruler himself was subject to not just active resistance but judgment and discipline—even deposition and execution—by the lesser estates for having acted the tyrant. More minor divides were delineated by such issues as: which criteria could lead to active resistance or rebellion; who were to be the principal agents or groups leading the resistance; the purpose of social compacts and national covenants, etc.

Further complicating any analysis of the Protestant resistance theories of this period is the fact that individual theologians often developed and changed their theories over time. For example, John Knox at first allowed only passive disobedience or flight, then within the next four years formulated the political theology which made it a positive duty to revolt against the "ungodly" ruler, and depose and execute him, by not only the nobility, but also the commoners.[8]

Besides Heinrich Bullinger (1504–1575), Zwingli's successor at Zurich,[9] John Calvin (1509–1564) remained the most conservative among the major Reformers, emphasizing obedience to political rulers and approving only passive disobedience to directives which were directly contrary to God's laws. Even in his private correspondence, he sounded the note of obedience.[10] Only in one section of his widely influential *Institutes of the Christian Religion* did he allow the possibility of a class of inferior magistrates revolting against a manifestly ungodly ruler—a distinctly aristocratic view.[11] But in some of his occasional minor works, Calvin did appear to support revolution on biblical grounds. For example, in his commentary on Daniel 6:22 (according to Puritan John Milton's 1649 translation), he declaimed: "Early princes depose themselves while they rise against God, yea they are unworthy to be numbered among men; rather it behooves us to spit upon their heads than to obey them."[12] Similarly, when preaching on the book of Daniel, Calvin declared that rulers who claim that God is not to be honored "are no longer worthy to be counted as princes," adding that "it is necessary that they should in turn be laid low."[13]

Huldrych Zwingli also attempted to maintain consistent adherence to the straightforward commands of St. Peter and St. Paul to give obedience to the ruling powers. However, even he could not ignore a biblical exception to political submission, when "such rulers . . . attack God's Word, or order preachers to distort the Word for their particular benefit." So, the only valid reason for rebellion would occur in a situation directly parallel to Acts 4. Zwingli allowed that in that situation, it would be "necessary to resist them, and, if needful, depose them, though without murder, war, or rebellion." But only the "whole people, or a large majority of the population," could depose the tyrant.[14] And, Zwingli warned, if Christians did not resist an ungodly tyrant, then they had to endure the tyrant and suffer God's ineluctable judgment.[15] From this warning, it is clear that Zwingli saw the people corporately responsible before God for the political corruption of their land. Perhaps his view of corporate responsibility contained the germ of a national covenant, but since he died in battle at a relatively young age, he left no mature statement of that kind of covenant.

RESISTANCE *IN EXTREMIS*

Armed resistance to most of the sixteenth century Reformers was a reaction to oppression *in extremis.* Even among those who acquiesced to allowing that response, the judgment was only grudgingly given. Martin Luther (1483–1546), as early as 1521 or 1522, had given standard arguments against insurrection, such as its causing more harm to the innocent than to the guilty. However, it seems that from about 1529 on, Luther became reconciled to the idea that the Reformation might be defended by force, "provided that active resistance was not offered to the Emperor himself." By 1539 Luther himself declared that the Pope was the Antichrist and had to be stopped at any cost. This was the only case that justified active resistance.[16] Thus, religious persecution was the only cause for which revolt was allowed.

Similarly, Luther's cohort, Philipp Melanchthon (1497–1560), did not support resistance in 1523, but he did take the position that a Christian prince could not stand by and watch innocents suffer. Rather, once a lesser prince was sure that a just cause existed and that it was God's will, war against the emperor was permitted. As late as 1532 he was still insisting on obedience as the normal response of the Christian to the magistrate.[17] In the 1536 opinion co-signed by Luther and others, Melanchthon held that the New Testament allowed all the protections allowed by natural law; in addition, princes were required to defend their subjects and the true Christian faith against "papist" idolatry.[18] Thus even here, the religious qualification is conditioned by reference to protections allowed by "natural law."

Another German Lutheran group, which the balance of current scholarly thought credits as the source of several strands of Reformed resistance theory, emphasized religious considerations as the *raison d'être* for their support of revolt.[19] After Catholic Emperor Charles V had attempted to stamp out Protestantism in Germany with the imposition of the Augsburg Interim, the city of Magdeburg refused to agree to the accord, incurring the emperor's ban. Niklaus von Amsdorf with Matthias Illyricus and seven other Lutheran pastors of Magdeburg authored a manifesto which, they declared, was based on the Scriptures, *rather than* on natural law or historical precedent. The Scriptures, they claimed, supported the position that if the "higher magistrate undertook by force to restore popish idolatry and to suppress or exterminate the pure teaching of the Holy Gospel . . . then the lower godfearing magistrate may defend himself and his subjects."

Significantly, not only were the "true teaching" and "worship of God" worth defending, but also the subject's "body, life, goods, and honor;"[20] i.e., economic and social considerations were to be taken into account along with the religious. While the pastors stressed the subjects' submission and obedience to authority in ordinary times, they reasoned that if, instead of protecting the good and persecuting evil—the *salus populi* of the ancients—rulers began "to persecute the good, they are no longer ordained of God."[21] Then the tyrants were to be removed from the special category of "higher powers," reduced to the status of private citizens and made liable to the penalties of private, positivistic law. These Lutherans also felt that if the emperor were to help the papacy, even he must be resisted by the lesser magistrates, since to help the Pope was to support the Antichrist.[22]

Another German Lutheran, Martin Bucer (1491–1551), began his exposition of the four Gospels by emphasizing the Christian's submission and obedience to the magistrate. While the private citizen was not to offer any resistance at all, the inferior magistrates, as well as kings, were "ordained of God" to ensure that the society lived according to God's will. And so, Bucer, arguing from the Old Testament, declared that lesser magistrates were to "preserve the people of God from evil and defend their safety and goods." Consequently, when the "superior power falls to extortion or causes any other kind of external injury," inferior magistrates in that system were to "attempt to remove him by force of arms."[23]

The first fully developed English theological work justifying resistance, *A Short Treatise of Politike Power*, was written by John Ponet (1514?–1556) in 1556. Although Ponet had been a bishop of the established church under Edward VI, his employment as pastor at Geneva indicates he was a staunch Calvinist.[24] Ponet argued that resistance against an ungodly magistrate was justified on biblical, historical, and natural philosophical grounds.[25] An ungodly magistrate was one who utterly neglected the reason for his dominion: the wealth of his own people.[26] Since all governors derived their authority from their subjects, the people might take back that authority, deposing unjust rulers. Indeed, governors were under the laws of God and natural law, and might be punished for their tyranny, "by the body of the hole congregacion or common wealthe."[27]

LESSER MAGISTRATES

The political thought of the sixteenth century was dominated by ideas of order and hierarchy, and even though the Reformers were challenging the theology and ecclesiastical structure of the Roman Catholic Church, their political theories were still constrained by conceptions of order and authority, as contrasted, in their minds, to those of the groups they considered anarchistic: the Anabaptists. Therefore, as they sought justifications for attempting to revolt against oppression, they could only seek for duly ordained authorities to challenge the oppressing authorities.

For example, in the first generation of Reformers, Melanchthon perceived the danger of anarchy resulting from private judgments as to self-defense, and emphasized the exclusive role of the lesser princes to lead insurrections. Eventually, he approved a private individual's right of resistance, but only when the ruler was unjust, illegitimate, and upheld the devil's order, i.e., Catholicism;[28] thus, religious oppression was a valid reason to revolt. Likewise, the German Lutheran pastors at Magdeburg could not see the populace as the agents of change. Calvin did allow a resistance movement to be led by the aristocracy of a country against the supreme sovereign, but his followers seized upon the lesser magistrate clause of his political theology and enlarged it all out of proportion to his dominant emphasis.[29] Nowhere had Calvin allowed revolt by private individuals: obedience remained the starting point for Reformed political ideology.

As Melanchthon had progressed beyond Luther's views concerning resistance to authority, so also did Theodore Beza (1519–1605), Calvin's chief aide and successor at Geneva, go beyond his mentor's. Although his major political work, *The Right of Magistrates*, appeared after the 1572 St. Bartholomew's Day Massacre of French Huguenots, it is clear that Beza had been thinking about resistance long before. In his 1554 *De haereticus a civili magistratu puniendis*, Beza mentioned, in the midst of his discussion about church and state, that a qualified resistance against a tyrant was legitimate, if carried out by lesser magistrates alone.[30] Beza continued that qualification in the 1560 version of the *Confession de la foy chrestienne*.[31] Anarchy apparently continued to be feared far more than severe autocracy.

Beza's *The Right of Magistrates*, published in 1574, explicitly justified armed resistance by inferior magistrates if a king broke his obligation to the purposes of government, but he warned that if individuals were allowed to revolt, "a thousand tyrants would arise on the pretext of suppressing one."[32] He still did not allow these magistrates to depose a sovereign from the throne.[33] In Scotland also, the doctrine of lesser magistrates continued to hold force. At least up to 1554, Knox approved only a revolt led by lesser magistrates against Catholics.[34]

But when Queen Mary I ascended the throne of England, she attempted to restore Catholicism, and unleashed a severe persecution of Reformed or Calvinistic Protestants, and in the process gave the impetus to what were some of the most radical Reformed justifications of revolution of the century. While some of the leading figures of the mid-century church in the British Isles were martyred, such as Hooper, Cranmer, Latimer, and Ridley, many others, armed with sharpened and poisoned pens, remained, including John Ponet and Christopher Goodman (1520–1603).

COVENANT

The Reformers after the initial generation developed intensively the idea of the covenant, not only of man-and-God relationships, but in applications to political arrangements. One of the most influential works on resistance in the French

Reformed community was a Huguenot work, *Vindiciae Contra Tyrannos* (1579), which was probably written by Philippe de Mornay. He held that the royal power was limited ethically by the law of God and politically by the whole people of a nation. Two covenants, made between God and king and between king and subjects, formed the constraints upon royal power.[35] In his perspective, the whole nation was jointly accountable to God for the purity of religious doctrine and worship.[36] And so, if idolatry should be introduced by the king, the whole people or an elite could give armed resistance to their sovereign; but again, no individual ought to lead a revolution.[37]

In England, Christopher Goodman straightforwardly justified revolution in his *How Superior Powers Ought to be Obeyed*. Since Goodman's arguments relied much more on biblical narratives than did Ponet's, Hildebrandt surmises that it "was written to refute scriptural objections which might have been raised to Ponet's theories."[38] Goodman not only showed from Old Testament examples that deposition and execution were legitimate responses of the *masses* against an ungodly government, but also that such a response was necessary. Otherwise, God would punish those who were merely inactive against sin, as well as those who were actually ungodly.[39] Sin in the form of governmental unrighteousness had to be resisted because, to Goodman, England was God's elect nation in covenant with Him. Because of that covenant, the people were charged to maintain all of God's laws.[40] The enduring influence of such thinking can be seen in the rigorous application of the national covenant model to Britain in Puritan sermons to Parliament in the period 1640–50. With the same resolve as Goodman, Ponet wrote that resistance against such evil was not only a possibility, but a positive duty for all citizens.[41] This position implied some sort of corporate obligation to God, or a covenant.

On the other hand, in Ponet's system, the private individual might lead a violent rebellion in two cases: where he had "som special inward commaundment or surely proved mocion of God" or "wher execucion of just punishment upon tirannes, idolaters, and traiterous governours is either by the hole state utterly neglected, or the prince with the nobilitie and counsail conspire the subversion or alteracion of their contery and people."[42] Ponet's book, on the other hand, was less radical than was Goodman's.

The resistance ideas of John Knox (1505–1572) not only followed the same general course of development as Reformed thinking overall, but also offered the most clearly delineated picture of the impact that the concept of a national covenant can work upon a theory of Christian armed resistance. It is especially pertinent to this monograph because of the influence Knox had on all subsequent churches of the Presbyterian strain, most notably the middle colony American Reformed clergy of the eighteenth century.

Until 1554, Knox counseled obedience to governmental authorities in all matters not contrary to God's express truths in Scripture; under the reign of Mary I (Bloody Mary), Knox advised his Reformed adherents to simply flee persecution if necessary; they were not to take up arms in their own defense.[43] In the four years between 1554 and 1558, Knox radically revised his position concerning revolution. His reputation for promoting radical resistance to ungodly rulers rests on three major works written in 1558: *First Blast of the Trumpet*; *Appelation to the Nobility*; and *Letter Addressed to the Commonality*. In *First Blast*, Knox put forth the proposition that the nobility, or lesser magistrates, were obliged to punish idolatry and blasphemy.[44] Hence, it was not only a right but a duty to violently resist "papist" rulers. Eventually Knox extended the duty to resist to the people of Scotland, and included in "resistance" the execution of the idolatrous queen and anyone who might hinder it.[45]

In the more narrowly directed *Appelation*, Knox required the nobility to protect the lives of their charges from ungodly rulers *and* bishops. Thus, Knox deemed general ecclesiastical reformation to be within the jurisdiction of the lesser civil magistrate.[46] Moreover, he placed responsibility for resisting the idolatrous ruler upon the commoners also, in an unusual merging of the doctrine of individual calling and the concept of the covenant community in a nation. Knox reasoned, "punishment of such crimes, as are idolatrie, blasphemie, and others that tuche the Majesty of God, dothe not appertaine to kinges and chefe rulers only, but also to the whole body of that people, and every member of the same, according to the vocation of everie man, and according to that possibilitie and occasion which God doth minister."[47] As Greaves observes, "Knox made it a sin . . . *not* to kill an idolatrous sovereign."[48] *All* Christians were bound in covenant with God to carry out its demands, including the duty to remove from their land that which they knew to be an abomination to God.[49]

Knox then addressed the commoners of Scotland, appealing to the doctrine of the spiritual equality of all believers.[50] Commoners had the right to "require" their superiors to "expell such as, under the name of pastours, devoure and destroy the flock." If such protection was not provided, then the populace most justly might "provide true teachers for yourselves . . . [who] maintaine and defend against all that shall persecute them . . . [and] withhold the frutes and profetts which your fals Byshoppes and Clergie most injustly receyve of you."[51]

But not all citizens of the nation were members of the Church or believers. Unlike Richard Hooker (1554–1600), Knox did not define members of the nation as members of the Church, merely by reason of their residing in the nation. Rather, the prophet approached the issue of a national church by means of the concept of the covenant. The people were in covenant with God, as were their rulers, and when reaching a sufficient proportion of the population of a nation, they were to carry out the stipulations of a national covenant, especially the suppression of sin. If the people of the covenant did not enforce the stipulations of the covenant, then they would stand condemned as covenant breakers.[52] No one was exempt from the covenant requirements, not even the king. Hence, Roman Catholic rulers, in introducing idolatry, were breaking the national covenant. Armed revolution became, in the Knoxian covenantal scheme, a requirement in the much larger, even cosmic, battle against sin.

The national covenant of Knox was worked out in later Scottish history, but especially in the 1643 Solemn League and Covenant at Westminster with English Reformed ministers. The idea of the national covenant, patterned after the Old Testament's theocratic covenant of Israel, became in this period cemented into Scottish Reformed and English Puritan thought. Throughout the seventeenth century, the idea of a national covenant provided one of the theological cornerstones for Reformed resistance ideology.

On the other hand, some of the traditional arguments against revolution lost many adherents during the course of the sixteenth century, at least in Reformed groups. Such tenets as the idea that bad government was a chastisement for the sins of the people satisfied almost no one. But the major pillars had been erected for Reformed resistance ideology. First, the threat of imposition of Catholicism became deeply ingrained as a legitimate basis for revolution, a position to reap a large scale harvest in the English civil war. Second, violation of the covenant of government between rulers and subjects became more widely accepted as a valid reason for resistance against tyrants. If the two preceding tenets are united with (1) a Knoxian national covenant to root out sin in its public forms and (2) the mythology of England as God's new elect nation, it can be seen that a compelling, though dormant, rationale already existed among the English-speaking peoples for a religiously justified revolution against tyranny.

NATURAL LAW OF SELF-DEFENSE

Alongside the justifications of revolution discussed above—i.e., religious oppression, the failure of rulers to carry out the very purpose for their office, the *salus populi*, and the accountability imposed on a people by a national covenant with God—throughout the pieces devoted to those justifications run appeals to the natural law of self-defense. Appeals to that law can be found, as well, throughout the works on resistance by the seventeenth century Puritans and those of the Calvinistic and Rhineland Reformed traditions of the European continent, to which the American colonial Presbyterians, the Dutch Reformed, the Baptists, and the German Reformed clergy were theologically indebted.[53] In the colonial theologians' writings there are definite ties between one use of natural law, the role of the magistrate, and resistance to tyranny. The foundation for their use of "natural law" is laid in the resistance writings of the Reformers of the sixteenth century.

The concept of natural law is nearly as old as Western intellectual history; the Greek philosophers, the Roman jurists and stoics, and the church fathers all formulated their own versions of natural law. The church fathers identified natural law as the "general and primitive law of mankind" given to Adam by God,[54] and Gratian's twelfth century *Decretum* posited that natural law was that law found in the "Scriptures and the Gospel."[55] However, it was Thomas Aquinas who developed the classic Roman Catholic position on natural law. Because "rational creatures" naturally have reason, they could discern and desire good and want to avoid evil; Aquinas defined the good as preeminently the preservation of human life, and legitimated as a proper means *self-defense*. Because sin had not invalidated the "essential principles of [human] nature," they could know natural law even if they could not completely fulfill the dictates of it.[56] Thus, in this world, human beings could develop a purely rational set of ethical standards and apply them, even if imperfectly, to social and political laws, movements, or institutions. Nevertheless, medieval Catholicism's natural law, as represented by Aquinas, was still not tainted by the proud autonomy of post-Reformation rationalism. Aquinas's view was inextricably tied to the divine nature of God and His providence. Man was not perfectible without revelation. There was still no salvation outside of Christ.[57]

In contrast to classic Catholic theology, Reformed theologians formulated a more pessimistic role for natural law, when considered in relation to the individual's salvation. Consistently throughout sixteenth and seventeenth century Reformed thought, natural law was subsumed within the moral law of the Bible.[58] God had directly "inscribed" or "imprinted" moral law on the "heart" of Adam and his offspring,[59] with the result that all human beings were accountable to God or "inexcusable" for their sins.[60] Inexcusability was integral to Reformed systems (even alongside the doctrines of election and depravity) because, though man's natural reason was "dimmed" or "cozened" by the Fall, "vestiges" of that natural law remained.[61] Human hearts had been so darkened that the written law of God was necessary to clarify God's will.[62] It was upon this basis that the Reformed clergy appealed directly to the Bible for political ethics; the written Word of God was the original natural law republished after the Fall.

Furthermore, natural law, according to Reformed perspectives, served to guide and restrain external behavior in society at large.[63] That law guided society through the agency of rulers and officials of government, as well as through ministers of the gospel. Calvin, Zwingli, Beza, and Bullinger (in his Second Helvetic Confession) all held the magistrate accountable for enforcement of both tables of the Decalogue, which, as shown before, was equated to the essence of natural law.[64] Along this same line the German Reformed Ursinus wrote:

> The law being engraven upon the minds and hearts of all men by God himself, speaking by the voice of ministers and magistrates, curbs and restrains even the unregenerate, so that they shun those flagrant and open forms of wickedness, which are in opposition to the judgment of sound reason as it utters itself even in persons unrenewed by the Spirit of God and which must be removed before regeneration.[65]

In tying the natural law to the actions of formal political officials via one of Reformed Protestantism's uses of natural law, Ursinus illustrated one of the primary routes by which Reformed theologians could justify their speaking to public affairs.

More politically inflammatory than the writings of Calvin, Zwingli, Bullinger, or Ursinus because of their explicit support for resistance were Theodore Beza's *The Rights of Magistrates* (1574), Bishop John Ponet's *A Shorte Treatise of Politike Power*, and *How Superior Powers Ought to be Obeyed* (1558) by English Calvinist Christopher Goodman. Goodman, relying primarily on biblical arguments and examples to justify resistance to oppression, argued that if Gentiles were taught self-preservation by "nature," and that if the law of nature was valid for the inferior creature, then it was legitimate for God's people to resist tyranny, especially if the tyrant was an instrument of the Pope.[66] To Ponet, rulers violating natural law, as seen in the biblical moral law, might be punished for their tyranny.[67] Beza's resistance tract, written after the slaughter of the Huguenots on St. Bartholomew's Day, uses natural law rhetoric more often, but his sundry arguments condense down into one: both human and divine law sanction self-defense.[68] In these Reformed systems, the magistrate guided peacetime society in light of natural law, but in addition, effected the defensive wars which natural law justified.[69]

Natural law remained, then, a continuing issue in Reformed theology. Within Reformed statements, three tenets recur in relation to natural law. First, natural law makes the unregenerate individual sufficiently knowledgeable of divine law so that he is inexcusable for violations of it. Indeed, inexcusability "may fairly claim to be a touchstone in assessing the fidelity of a theologian to the Reformed tradition."[70] Natural law was impotent to help morally crippled man toward salvation except by convicting him of sin. Second, the substance of natural law could accurately be found only in the moral law of the Scriptures, distilled in the Decalogue and in rightly reasoned extrapolations from the Two Tables. Lastly, natural law was useful to guide and oversee the socio-political order containing both "wheat and tares." Reformed theology legitimated armed resistance to oppression through the political order, with the natural law of self-defense of the individual actually being at the base of that legitimation.

From the above sketch of sixteenth century Reformed resistance writings, a number of generalizations can be formed. First, Reformed theologians and ministers all started from and emphasized the biblical injunction of obedience to political authorities. Second, passive disobedience was always required in response to commands of rulers that were obviously against God's laws. Third, a progression in responses to tyranny can be observed: from obedience, to more allowances for disobedience, to armed combat. Fourth, armed resistance was primarily allowed when oppression was religious in nature, i.e., when a ruler attempted to enforce observance of Catholicism. Fifth, the aristocracy was considered to be the prime agent in control of ungodly, oppressive rulers. Last, all the subjects of a nation were held responsible before God for allowing corruption to be perpetuated in the land, especially if both the king and the lesser magistrates abdicated their responsibilities of ensuring observance of God's law. The idea of a corporate or national covenant underlying this perspective became much clearer in John Knox's resistance theory of the sixteenth century, and even more so in that of the English-speaking Puritans of the seventeenth century.

2

War, Revolution, and the Puritan Clergy

Between the Reformation and the American Revolution lay the English civil war and the crucial expansion of orthodox Puritanism. When Puritan politico-religious ideas are examined, it can be seen that a number of concepts employed by sixteenth century Reformed divines and developed by the Puritans were later taken up and utilized to argue resistance against the restored British Crown. It will be apparent that the same set of theological principles of the Puritan clergy which upheld a submission-to-higher-powers ethic in peaceful times, also impelled them to resist those powers in times of oppression; this theological ethic they based squarely on the Bible. The American middle colony Reformed clergy built their eighteenth century evangelical theology upon the Puritan and Reformed faiths of the seventeenth century and retained the potential for violent resistance, while holding to the norm of submission to governmental authority.

In fact, the revolutionary propensities of sixteenth and seventeenth century Calvinistic Protestantism, especially of the English Puritans, have been magnified in modern historiography, almost to the point of misrepresentation. Puritanism served overall as a conservative force,[1] while retaining a potentiality for explosive resistance to oppression.[2] But to a man, the Puritan preachers were more than prepared to preach a just war to prevent the capture of England by forces of their Antichrist, the Pope, and under a combination of just war theory, anti-Catholicism, and the elect nation ideology, they were moved to support revolution by the Long Parliament, recoiling, too late, from the execution of the king.[3] In the eighteenth century, a similar conjunction of just war sentiments and a chosen nation ideology motivated the heirs of the Puritans, the colonial Reformed clergy, to preach revolution against the British Crown.

PURITAN CHRISTENDOM

In the seventeenth century, the fundamental premise of the Puritan divines as well as their predecessors with regard to political authority was consistently conservative: the Christian owed the magistrate obedience in all things unless otherwise directed by the Word of God.[4] The crucial question, though, is: was there a point at which a political constraint ceased to be a matter of indifference and required a response of armed resistance? To understand what it was in their perceptions that decided that boundary, two groups of ideas must be examined: (1) the ideas they held in continuity with the Reformed tradition, i.e., their general political theory, the Christian state, natural law, just war theory, and fear of Catholicism; and (2) the peculiarities of their thought or its application to their circumstances, i.e., elect nation ideology, millennialism, and fear of Arminianism, and the evil men or malignants theory.[5]

As with Christian preachers in all ages, the Puritan divines had assumed many of the ideas of their predecessors. Along with the rest of the Christian world of the seventeenth century, they approved without hesitation the conception of the *corpus christianum* or the Christian state.[6] In that kind of nation, the state exercised what today would be considered an obvious religious function: the enforcement of the Two Tables of the Decalogue or the Ten Commandments—that is, the basic duties of men to God and to one another. The Christian state was to restrain sin, most especially idolatry,[7] to protect the church, and to further the Gospel.[8]

However, the *corpus christianum* of these Puritans was a Protestant *corpus;* public promotion of the Roman Catholic religion could not be tolerated. Indeed, many, if not most, of the Puritan divines on both sides of the Atlantic were sure that heretical, non-Catholic groups such as the Quakers ought not be tolerated in the pure Christian state.[9] For these Puritan divines, government received its authority directly from God, an idea which made every rebel against a lawful government a rebel against God.[10] God had ordained government, but the forms of every human government could vary with each particular nation.[11] Mixed constitutional monarchy formed the best arrangement for the English, but because the Scriptures gave no divine plan for governmental forms, the Puritans refused to specify any particular form as the right form.[12]

One of the immutable principles of Puritan political beliefs was that God had ordained government for the good of the people, i.e., the *salus populi* of the ancients' natural law.[13] Indeed, again and again, for the Puritan ministers the only valid government was a "just" one, with the object of that justice being the mass of the people.[14] That no one might take away another's life or goods without good cause formed the fundamental principle of justice.[15] This fundamental, commonsense evaluation was held to not only by the New

England Puritans and John Locke, but later also by the eighteenth century colonial Reformed divines. Such a pervasive adherence indicates the enduring power of the *salus populi* tenet to command assent, as well as its revolutionary use against absolutism. Furthermore, an absolute monarchy could never be countenanced, for England's people in some sense had created, in compact with each other, a limited monarchy.[16] However, the compact for government in the writings of these divines may not have been necessarily a Lockean kind of compact,[17] nor was government envisioned as solely a creature of the masses. In any case, regardless of how constitutional the government may have been, the Word of God set limits on any human authority, including sovereigns.[18] So, the existence of government was divinely ordained, but not its form.

Beyond receiving a common heritage of the *corpus christianum* and the *salus populi*, the Puritans also shared a common attitude towards the use of the state to support the program of the true church. The state, if it was a Christian state, must have some measure of control over the external religious lives of its subjects, even if not over their consciences. Unrestrained religious freedom would invite heresy, impiety, and even anarchy.[19]

But control of religion by the state had its limits, and leading Independent John Owen consistently condemned any forced uniformity of the saints;[20] yet, he declared to Parliament that "popish" religion "cannot upon our concessions plead forbearance." In addition, he argued more generally that the state should proceed with the sword against all who propagate opinions against basic doctrines of Christianity: "such expressions or . . . acts, as are fit to power contempt and scorn upon the truth."[21] To insist that society, through the agency of government, had to suppress certain ideas about religious belief implied some sort of accountability to God to do so, or some sort of covenant-keeping to avoid judgment. God, they believed, had a covenant with Protestant Britain.

In sum, the Puritans held to the centuries-old ideal of the Christian state, i.e., the two-swords concept which said that church and state governed the nation to enforce upon it the will of God. Because Britain was a Protestant Christian state, the state was to protect and further the mission of the Protestant Christian religion. On the other hand, the state was also open to censure by the church, for absolute monarchy could not be condoned by Christians: God alone was absolute, and human governments were limited by His laws, a fundamental one being that the state existed for the good of its subjects.

JUST WAR AND NATURAL LAW

The theory of the just war constituted another major element of the intellectual inheritance of the Puritans. This centuries-old western tradition condoned a limited war in defense of the Christian state, as did the historically closer Protestant and English church traditions. One section of the 1571 Thirty-Nine Articles plainly approved the just war,[22] and the Puritans' own 1647 Westminster Confession did not differ essentially from the Articles: "It is lawful for Christians . . . now under the New Testament, [to] wage war upon just and necessary occasion."[23] But these creeds did not define "just," nor did they distinguish revolution from war.

On the other hand, Westminster divine John Ley, preaching to the House of Commons in 1643, did set out concise constraints to a just war. After summarizing the evils of war and civil war, Ley confirmed its lawfulness[24] because the Scriptures did also: the "holiest and most accepted by God" in the Old Testament were warriors, and in the New Testament the soldiers were not condemned by John the Baptist and the faith of the Roman centurion Cornelius was praised. Furthermore, the New Testament had set up the magistrate with the sword "not only against one single offender, but against many . . . if there be military force raised to hinder justice." In addition to the Bible, "the light of nature" approved armed self-defense not only between individuals, but between groups also, if one group was defending their "lives, Lawes, Liberties, and Estates." Lastly, Ley adduced proof of the legality of war from church history, citing Tertullian, Eusebius, and Augustine as his authorities.[25]

Six conditions had to be met before war could be considered legitimate. First, "a" lawful authority had to initiate the war. Second, the cause had to be "weighty" and "just." Third, such a war had to be fought for a good end, i.e., so that the subjects "may lead a peaceable and quiet life, in all godliness and honesty." Fourth, not only the end but also the means must be good: noncombatants must be spared, and not robbed.[26] Fifth, war could not be undertaken until all other means were exhausted. Lastly, once peace was concluded, all fighting must stop. Ley inferred on the basis of Judges 5:23 and Jeremiah 48:10 that a war meeting all these criteria could not be *un*just. Given the above constraints on war, "to forebear it is unlawful," for if an enemy is not given violence for violence, "a worse thing then warre will follow . . . perpetuall tyranny and slavery upon the consciences and persons of the vanquished." Ley concluded, as others have since, that "a noble death is much rather to be chosen then an ignominious and miserable life."[27] What is significant about this listing of just war criteria is that all of them can be paralleled in eighteenth century New England Congregational preaching and middle colony Reformed preaching as well, as will be discussed later.

Dovetailed with the concept of the just war is the complex of ideas commonly called natural law. In Puritanism, the English-American version of Reformed Christianity, an all-encompassing attempt was made to regulate the whole of life by the biblical commandments of God. Law *per se* held a central place in Puritan thought, but the Puritan view of natural law was *not* derived from rationalistic philosophy. John Eusden wrote:

> The Puritans and the lawyers had their higher law, but it was not reason. It was divine sovereignty and fundamental law. The Puritans and the lawyers believed in an English *civitas* governed by God and law; their higher law was an other-worldly, commanding rule.

In contrast, "the natural law thinkers . . . envisioned their higher law as a rational model . . . to which actual existence conformed and on which the good society . . . must be constructed."[28]

Natural law or reason, when *rightly* used, coincided with the law of God, according to the Puritans.[29] As the esteemed William Ames wrote in *The Marrow of Sacred Divinity*: "That which is said to be right reason, if absolute rectitude be looked after, is not elsewhere to be sought for then where it is, that is, in the Scriptures: neither doth it differ from the will of God revealed for the direction of our life."[30] The Puritans agreed, along with the sixteenth century Reformed thinkers, that knowledge of natural law was dimmed by the Fall, and that the ability to obey that law was crippled. But, even though clouding mind and maiming ability, those debilities were neither complete nor absolute.[31] Therefore both king and peasant alike were accountable to carry out the dictates of the natural law.[32] And, in regards to that accountability, Samuel Rutherford wrote that since self-preservation was part of the natural law,[33] when the king transgressed that natural or "fundamental" law, then resistance to him was a permissible conformity to it.[34]

Rutherford's contemporary William Ames illustrates what has been shown of Reformed thinkers in general concerning natural law and the biblical moral law with regards to political ethics. To Ames, both God's law and natural law upheld the justice of defensive armed resistance. The illustration here consists not in his position, but in his argumentation. Ames does not argue this statement with rational propositions and logic, but rather cites several Scriptures and draws his conclusions from them.[35]

The New England Puritans of the first generation were English-born and trained, and the creed for both Old and New World Puritans was the Westminster Confession (1647), "by far the most important confessional witness in American colonial history."[36] In it the basic points of Puritan thinking on natural law were creedalized. It asserted that the magistrate was to enforce God's ordinances and to protect the church from injury;[37] it affirmed other basic Reformed positions on natural law and condoned defensive war. Although their great migration to America occurred in the two decades prior to the Westminster Confession, the Puritans brought with them essentially the same Westminster covenant theology, and Massachusetts sermonic literature shows that the seventeenth and eighteenth century New England Reformed clergy carried on the same perspectives on natural law as their predecessors.

While it might seem that the eighteenth century New England heirs to the Puritans drew more frequently upon Aristotle, Plato, Cicero, Locke, Pufendorf, Milton, and Harrington for their political philosophy, resulting in a "greatly extended use of natural law" of "a more secular and more philosophical conception" than before,[38] it is doubtful whether most of the New England Puritans threw over the classic Reformed subsumption of natural law under the law of God.

Published election day sermons of the New England divines in both the seventeenth and eighteenth centuries display classic Reformed perspectives on natural law.[39] For example, Harvard graduate Jonathan Mitchell (1624–1668) stated in an election sermon of 1667 that "that is indeed the Law of Nature, is a part of the Eternal Law of God." To Mitchell, the Roman maxim *salus populi suprema lex* was a natural law; thus it was "owned and confirmed by the Scriptures . . . and it is easily deducible from the Law of God" because "the Law of God enjoyns, that in Humane Civil Affairs, things be managed according to right Reason and Equity." Notably, though he reasoned by logic, he cited as his authority Romans 13:14.[40] This demonstrates that for Mitchell, the Scriptures had to be the center of focus for divine guidance even in civil affairs, because natural law had become unusable due to the depravity and darkening of the human soul.

Toward the end of the seventeenth century, one-time vice president of Harvard University Samuel Willard (1640–1707) played a leading role in conserving orthodox Puritan theology by summarizing the Westminster Catechism in a series of catechetical lectures. In the lectures on the fifth commandment, Willard said that natural law worked in two ways. First, natural law functioned mainly to make man inexcusable for his transgressions against a holy God.[41] Second, natural law for people in community worked to "keep them in awe and prompt them to duty," and to preserve "civil Societies from Ruin." Thus, in general it was useful to direct mankind, both rulers and ruled, in ordering political society.[42] Obviously, for Willard the natural law for societies was subsumed under the fifth commandment. According to the moral law of the fifth commmandment, defensive war, and even aspects of offensive war, were legitimate.

To Willard (in words the middle colony revivalist Gilbert Tennent later repeated), "Self-preservation is a principle so closely rivetted into the Nature of the Creatures that it is unnatural to doubt the Lawfulness of it." To decide to be oppressed rather than "to stand on our Defense, and resist an injurious

Adversary, is to forego Reason itself." Thus, war—a corporate response—was actually based on the natural law of self-defense found in individual creatures, but the execution of warfare devolved onto the responsibility and authority of magistrates, for "they ought to vindicate the Affronts and Injuries offered their Persons or [their] subjects' " life or property. Civil insurrections, on the other hand, Willard hotly condemned.[43]

Willard's recapitulation of Puritan theology remained a standard position for most Reformed ministers. Nonetheless, by the end of the seventeenth century the Puritan socio-religious system faced serious challenges brought about by increased affluence and by the intellectual perspectives of the Enlightenment. New voices were being raised in the eighteenth century, especially concerning the relationship of church and state, and man's capabilities and place in the universe. One work indicative of those newer trends, which was proved enduringly popular by its reprinting just prior to the Revolutionary War, was John Wise's 1717 *Vindication of the Government of New-England Churches.* Wise (1652–1725), in attempting to defend New England Congregationalism, revised Reformed theology in some important respects, using in the process not so much biblical texts for his authorities as Aristotle, Plato, Plutarch, and Pufendorf. Government became not a divine institution, but one formed by "Humane Free-Compacts." The law of nature and revelation were equally "an Emanation of his [God's] Wisdom," and, thus, were to be trusted equally in devising political arrangements. Wise was prudent enough, though, to say that "Revelation is Natures Law in a fairer and brighter Edition."[44]

But even into the mid-eighteenth century the majority of the Puritans maintained the subsumption of natural law under the moral law of the Bible. Representative of the bulk of New England Congregationalists in their approach to natural law and public affairs was John Barnard (1681–1770), a moderate Calvinist. Barnard perceived natural law in essentially the same way as that of his forerunner Jonathan Mitchell: things might be properly reasoned out by men, but the authority of the Scriptures remained the sole canon by which the natural law is confirmed and clarified. In a 1734 election sermon, Barnard declared that government had the "stamp of the Divine authority upon it" and that it came to men "with a *thus saith the Lord."* God may have "taught" government "to Mankind, by the Light of natural Reason," but He "plainly required it, in His holy Word."[45] Harry Stout observes that even into the Revolutionary period New England Congregationalists held to the priority of the Scriptures over natural revelation, even if they did wrest both political and spiritual meanings from biblical texts by a hermeneutical maneuver called "double extractions."[46]

IDEOLOGICAL DISCONTINUITIES

In addition to the older ideas of the Christian state, natural law, and the just war, Puritan teachers inherited an identification of Britain with Old Testament Israel, God's elect nation, probably under the influence of John Foxe's 1563 *Book of Martyrs.*[47] They continued this nationalistic identification into the Interregnum period,[48] and perhaps more importantly for eighteenth century political developments, Puritans crossing the Atlantic during the Laudian persecutions carried with them the identification of the *Puritan* Church with Israel to New England. This identification became intimately bound up with their eschatology.

Although the foundations of the millennial fears and hopes that pervaded seventeenth century Britain were inherited from their sixteenth century predecessors, the Puritan clergy began to shift from the typical Protestant eschatology to an apocalyptic or millenarian orientation. Though the Puritans' eschatological perspective started from the Reformed identification of the Pope with the Antichrist,[49] many Puritans of this period went beyond their own Westminster Confession, for they believed that they were living in the biblical last days in which the Antichrist and the Beast were to be destroyed at Christ's return. These last days had been inaugurated by the Protestant Reformation,[50] and the success of the Protestant movement in both Europe and the New World between 1588 and 1700 confirmed their last days' perceptions, regardless of whether they were postmillennial or amillennial in their persuasions.[51] The intensified millennial expectations—i.e., the apocalypticism of the 1630–60 period—added urgency to a number of attitudes and movements in which the Puritans participated, from the civil wars, to missions, to anti-Catholicism. This apocalypticism constituted a discontinuity with their common Protestant eschatology.

While apocalypticism acted as a catalyst to intensify the perceptions and reactions of the Puritan clergy toward a number of developments, the fear of national conquest by Roman Catholicism and its adherent nations formed the strongest motivation for revolution for not only the Puritan clergy but, as Finlayson has so persuasively argued, all English Protestants.[52] One of the hallmarks of English nationalism was, according to Robin Clifton, anti-Catholicism.[53] However, the Puritan clergy saw the Arminianism of the established Church hierarchy not only as tending towards heresy, but also as the precursor to popery. Probably all Puritan clergymen would have agreed with the vivid interpretation of a hypothetical Arminian's connections by unordained Francis Rous, a lay member of the Westminster Assembly. He declared:

> an Arminian is the spawn of a Papist; and if there come the warmth of favour upon him, you shall see him turn into one of those frogs that rise out of the

bottomless pit. And if you mark it well, you shall see an Arminian reaching out his hand to a Papist, a Papist to a Jesuit, a Jesuit gives one hand to the Pope and the other to the King of Spain; these men having kindled a fire in our neighbor country, now they have brought over some of it hither, to inflame this Kingdom also.[54]

This kind of thinking indicates how the rising intensity of almost paranoid anti-Catholicism in the third, fourth, and fifth decades increased the number of local tumults and helped trigger the civil wars themselves.[55] Ardent Puritan anti-Catholicism, with its associated suspicion of High Church Anglicanism, developed into a near-permanent feature of Reformed Christianity (especially via chapter 25, section 6 of the Westminster Confession) for the next 250 years. Certainly, the middle colony Reformed clergy in the eighteenth century were horrified by the latitudinarianism of the established British church.

Significantly, during the Restoration references to the Antichrist decrease, implying a loss of apocalyptic urgency. Since the Anglican church was being reestablished by their restored king and by the Parliament with which they had thrown in their lot during the civil war, the Puritan preachers were no longer able to determine with certainty whether the established church or the king were the tools of the Antichrist. If the Antichrist could not with certainty be identified, then no minister could preach the imminent overthrow of the Antichrist. This decrease in references to the Antichrist in the Restoration supports the thesis that a magnified fear of Catholicism, in combination with the elect nation ideology, edged the Puritan clergy toward revolution, and away from their normal Christian position of submission to higher powers.[56]

MALIGNANT FACTION THEORY

The Puritan preachers accepted just war first on the basis of Scripture, primarily the Old Testament, and secondarily on their version of natural law. But Puritan arguments for defensive war or revolution using natural law rhetoric were supported by Scripture citations. Civil war they resolved into the just war category by asserting that, in reality, they warred against a malignant court faction dominated by papists with foreign loyalties, who had in some way gained control of the king. These Puritans wished to rid the country of this vaguely defined malignant faction and *return* the government to what they perceived as the *status quo* before the revolution. Notably, this was also the stated motivation of the American middle colony Reformed clergy in the period 1774–76, as discussed later.

The members of this court faction advising the king were, if not secret agents for the Pope, then at least inclined towards popery and corruption, intentionally sowing the seeds of division and dissent in Britain. They were labeled the "malignant party," who had "misled" the king, or "seduced" him to commit the injustices he had perpetrated against the people of England. They were, as Puritan preachers commonly described them, "Jesuits and Papists, and Atheists, . . . with Cavaliers." Now, however tenuous this malignant party theory may have become as the civil war decade wore on, it must have held sway in the perceptions of the Puritan clergy, for examples could be multiplied of Puritan sermons supporting a qualified just war against the king's court and messengers, but rarely, if ever, against the king himself.[57]

One typical example was Independent John Goodwin, who, in his 1642 sermon *Anticavalierisme*, cited "the manifest Law of God, and the common light of nature" as his authorities for standing up

> in defense of your lives, your Liberties, your Estates . . . in defense of those Religious and faithful Governours, that Honourable Assembly of Parliament . . . Yea, in defense of his Majesties royall person, honour, and estate; all of which are now in eminent danger to suffer by that accursed retinue of vile persons that are gathered about him, as Ivie about an Oake, which never suffers it to thrive or prosper, till it be torne off from it.[58]

Against Catholic sympathizers Goodwin upheld the "true Protestant Religion" as a just object for defense. But when arguing the question of armed resistance against an unjust command of a king, he talked relatively little about the law of nature; rather, the bulk of his argumentation was taken up by Old Testament biblical examples. For Goodwin and the other Puritan preachers, revolution was to be subsumed under the just war when the king's commands—especially if they were motivated by the "malignant faction" of courtiers about him—threatened the lives or property of law-abiding men and women.[59]

Again, Thomas Hill, when preaching one of the institutionalized sermons to Parliament, validated civil war because the instigators of it were the papists, the "malignants," who "illegally invade our persons, Religion, and . . . our birthright." Although this sermon was dominated by an expectant millennialism, Hill did not exhort the saints to take up arms to destroy the forces of the Antichrist, as vivid as the military images are that he presented. Rather, he spiritualized the conflict by declaring that "for the overcomming of popery, we need not other weapons to consume it, but the Spirit" and "word of their testimony." Because paganism, Islam, and popery were nothing but a "heape of grosse mistakes raised in the dark, . . . spirituall weapons [must] . . . cast downe the strong holds of the Devil." However, it is probably doubtful whether he would have eschewed the use of an old-fashioned halberd as secondary means to further the demolition.⁶⁰

In view of the continuities and discontinuities above, the revolutionary resistance ideology of the Interregnum period, which is not apparent after the Restoration, should be viewed as an aberration from normal, i.e., peacetime, Puritan beliefs. Even though war was not greatly difficult for Puritans to justify, revolution *was*,⁶¹ for the norm of Calvinistic Protestantism was submission to governmental authorities. The Puritan divines did not or could not see, as the sixteenth century Huguenots were forced to see, that it was the king himself who was against them and their potent political alliance with parliamentarians and lawyers. The Huguenots had to face reality because their Protestant royal hope converted to popery before their eyes; the Puritans' king was executed before they allowed themselves the realization that he was a tyrant.

The malignant party construction allowed the Puritan ministers to hold both to their theological ethic of submission to political authority, and to their personal allegiance to the king as Englishmen. The malignants theory deformed their political preaching toward militant resistance, not because it was the theory most plausible (for some of their compatriots shortly saw through the fiction),⁶² but because it was stoked by the elect nation ideology,⁶³ by the just war theory, and by a heightened millennialism wherein Roman Catholicism headed by the Pope was the Antichrist.

Because the Puritans saw their own era as the last days in which all who did not join with God in crushing the Beast would be crushed themselves,⁶⁴ it behooved them to resist any incursion of papal influence into their nation. Because they perceived Roman Catholicism as an invasion of a foreign political power, as well as a foreign, heretical religion (even then oppressing their Reformed brethren on the Continent), revolution to them became a just war against an invader. The king himself, or monarchy as such, was exempt from attack, except to a few radical republicans. Even then, most resistance statements were not for *armed* resistance, but rather more on the order of civil disobedience.⁶⁵

When faced with the possibility that the dissemination of the true faith would be restrained, or even worse, that their elect, covenanted nation would be handed back to the Romanists through the agency of the High Church henchmen, the Puritan preachers called upon all within their intellectual repertoire to support resistance. The forward progress of the faith, especially through preaching, was absolutely crucial to these men, and whatever opposed that progress was indeed the enemy and, of necessity, had to be opposed. The heirs of Puritanism, the New England Congregationalists and the middle colony Reformed clergy, assumed the same attitude in the eighteenth century when preaching revolution against Britain.

NEW ENGLAND RESISTANCE IDEOLOGY

The New England Congregationalists constituted the ideological bridge from the English Puritans to the middle colony Reformed clergy, and in broad brush strokes the New Englanders held to the same political ethics as their English and Scottish counterparts. Both old and New England Puritans held to the *salus populi* as the divinely ordained purpose of government, saw natural law as found in biblical moral law to be a valid guide to political ethics, agreed that the church was to be maintained and protected by the state (e.g., Westminster Confession and Cambridge Platform),[66] and taught that the first response of the Christian towards government was submission. However, the master key to comprehending New England preaching on political themes is to be found in their use of the concept of the covenant, which follows the framework constructed by Knox as discussed earlier.[67]

All civil relationships for the New World Puritans and their eighteenth century heirs came about through covenants. For example, John Cotton, a leading Bay Colony preacher of the first generation of American Puritans, wrote: "all civil relations are founded in Covenant. . . . There is no other way whereby a people . . . free from natural and compulsory engagements, can be united or combined together in one visible body . . . but only by mutual covenant," regardless of whether those relationships were in the family, the city, or the commonwealth.[68] That attitude was reinforced by their historical experience in largely homogeneous, small New England communities.

Of course, the Puritans of New England recognized that these external social covenants were voluntary associations (as contrasted to the internal irresistable covenant between God and the individual); mutual consent was required for the parties involved in the former. In consequence, those not desiring to join the church did not have to do so, and those not wanting to submit to the laws and mores of the Puritan communities were free to leave.[69] Since the New England clergy conceived themselves as keepers of the covenant with God, they had to see to it that both Tables of the Decalogue were enforced in order to prevent moral decay from destroying their New Israel, for God would hold the whole colony accountable for the actions of even a few unrighteous, believers or not.[70] Magistrates as well as ministers were to be especially pure to maintain a godly commonwealth.

On the other hand, by the end of the seventeenth century, the strictness of the Puritans' attempts to maintain the purity of both church and state had corroded, and with that loss a shift had occurred: the criteria by which a magistrate could be removed or be rebelled against had changed. In the late seventeenth and early eighteenth centuries, the criteria had been changed from personal moral fitness to govern to an emphasis on how well the magistrate protected material or property rights of the governed. "Fundamental law" formed the parameters for those material, temporal rights; that law placed absolute limits on all human authority.

Fundamental law was, furthermore, the biblical commandments, an absolute standard of right and wrong.[71] The belief that God alone wielded an absolute authority constituted the bedrock foundation of fundamental law. More specifically, the New England Congregationalists in this period believed that the fundamental law posited criteria countenancing rebellion against political authority. For example, Samuel Nowell in the 1680s declared that New Englanders could revolt against those who confiscated their property without cause; of course this echoes the earlier Puritans of old England.[72] Nowell warned, furthermore, that "the law of nature . . . teacheth self-preservation," and if "Liberty and property . . . are invaded, we may defend ourselves."[73]

This is not to say that religion had been dropped from the reasons to revolt; after the turn of the century both the conservative Ebenezer Pemberton and the more radical John Wise wrote that rebellion could be condoned if the "fundamental constitution" or the "fundamental laws of society were subverted by governors"; i.e., if "laws and liberties, religion and properties" were attacked.[74] Breen observes that in the last decades of the seventeenth century *magistrates* had begun to cite reason and experience rather than Scripture to substantiate their actions; e.g., rebellion against Governor Andros was justified not because he tried to introduce idolatry into the colony (Catholicism) but because he attacked the colonists' rights of property and liberty. But after 1690, even the ministerial Mathers "in effect infused property with a sacred quality and then proceeded to defend it with an evangelical fervor once reserved only for the Church itself."[75]

In mid-eighteenth century New England, Congregationalists preached that revolt against those rulers who violated fundamental law was legitimate, with the dominant conceptual framework continuing to be the covenant. Stout writes that, after the "Rubicon" was crossed—i.e., the decision to revolt against Britain—the New England clergy began to downplay the themes of New England's exclusive covenant, which had played so vital a part in earlier war preaching, for example, in Jonathan Edwards's mid-century sermons.[76] God had, they declared, upheld the liberty of his covenant people throughout the past generations, and would continue to do so while they kept his covenant. Of course, this covenant was modeled after the Old Testament covenant with Israel, and Old Testament sermon texts provided the precedents for revolution, especially as they were drawn from the period of the Divided Kingdom. Once the American Revolution had actually started, the New England clergy broadened the covenant to include all of colonial America.[77]

Invocations of the just war for the covenant people seem just as ubiquitous in the eighteenth century as in the seventeenth. By reducing the British authorities (the king or Parliament) to nonmagistrates on account of their tyrannous intergovernmental actions (e.g., colonial taxation) which were on the level of violations of individual persons (e.g., robbery or murder),[78] the New England clergy were able to claim that natural rights were violated; then self-defense became legitimate, including armed combat. Thus fundamental law was violated, and the covenant transgressed because covenantal thinking required consent of the governed.

Since the issue of strict Reformed religion in a godly commonwealth was now being played *piano,* and since property and political liberty were of concern to all colonists, and since New England sermons for resistance were designed to mobilize the unchurched masses, appeals to those common concerns would naturally be highlighted. In the same way, the inclusion of all the colonies in a national covenant would not only strike deep chords in the hearts of those with a similar covenantal mind-set—i.e., middle colony Scots-Irish Presbyterians—but also would engage those commercial and political factions seeking protection or autonomy for their interests, for example, the southern planters.

Just as important as the above to the development of revolutionary sentiment, according to a fair number of scholars, were the effects of the Great Awakening upon the society at large. These researchers argue that by providing a common spiritual experience, the Awakening produced in all the colonies an increased self-consciousness and a unified perception of themselves as distinct from other countries. Because the revivalists, in resolutely carrying on with the work of God, did not hesitate to attack the status quo among church members and ministers, they prepared the awakened ones to challenge the Parliament and eventually the British Crown.[79]

The commitment of the New England clergy and colonists to the king ultimately collapsed and was pushed to the "periphery" of their value system in favor of the above central values.[80] In view of the fact that New England preceded the other divided colonies in making the transition from submissive subjects to radical revolutionaries, it can be persuasively argued that the "religious underpinnings of Revolutionary rhetoric in the New England pulpit help to explain why the momentous shift from constitutional monarchy to republican government occurred" so quickly and easily.[81] While Reformed preaching of resistance in the middle colonies may not have been as soon or as certain, at least at first, it eventually did spur on the colonists there to a "just" resistance. This preaching was based both on continuities with older Reformed theology and resistance ideology, and the adaptation of those ideas to the totally new situation in colonial America; investigation of those factors will constitute the remaining chapters of this monograph.

3

From Awakening to War

The political-religious war ideology of Reformed, English-speaking Protestantism came to its fullest and most fateful application during the middle decades of the eighteenth century in America. Not only in New England, under the strident harangues of the Congregational "black regiment," but also in the middle colonies, in response to the inducements of Presbyterian, Dutch Reformed, German Reformed, and Baptist clergymen, Christians and non-Christians alike took up arms to defend their lives, property, and religion, first against the French, and later against the British.

On the one hand, these colonial ministers built on the centuries-old theory of the just war and straightforwardly appealed to the natural law of self-defense, and ideas of justice, government, and covenant, theologically extracted from the Bible. On the other hand, their New World experience stimulated the application of those concepts supporting resistance in ways that were discontinuous with historical Reformed thought. The middle colony Reformed clergy appropriated the New England Puritan idea of an elect nation after the two most powerful phenomena of the mid-eighteenth century: the Great Awakening and the French and Indian wars. The former had shaken the religious status quo in all the colonies; in a perceptual sense, it had democratized salvation, and in the process given the colonists a common spiritual experience that ultimately undermined hierarchical social authority.[1] Fighting in the mid-century wars against the Catholic French had given the American colonists another common experience—combat; and this in turn had enhanced their self-perception as Americans, instead of just British colonists. The middle colony Reformed preachers and theologians in the period of 1740 to 1781 took the concept of the elect, covenanted nation and reapplied it from England which had forfeited it, then to New England, then to the pluralistic middle colonies and all of America. The New Jerusalem, the city set upon a hill by God for salvation, was extended beyond New England to all colonial America.

Even though the middle colony Reformed tenaciously maintained their loyalty to the British Crown until 1776, once war came they chose armed resistance. In their understanding, civil and religious liberties were maintained or lost together; to them, war was necessary to prevent the attempt of a corrupt, Arminian nation to thwart the manifest religious destiny of America.

What makes this reapplication and extension of that concept so anomalous is the milieu in which they were carried out, against the backdrop of the theology the middle colony Reformed clergy preached in all of their non-political sermons: i.e., the consistent calls for repentence and salvation of the elect. Such an application in New England, might almost be comprehensible for its ecclesiastical landscape was totally dominated by Congregationalists entrenched in established churches within culturally homogeneous British colonies, but Protestantism in the middle colonies was a melange of competing groups—sometimes hostile, sometimes tolerant, and sometimes cooperative historic churches and new sects. There were no truly established churches in the middle colonies; the Anglicans held only a legal pretense to establishment in New York, and economic-political influence alone was wielded by such church groups as the Quakers in Pennsylvania. The Great Awakening ecclesiastically splintered most of the already fragmented middle colony churches, adding to the preexisting theological diversity and further undermining any possibility of establishment.[2]

Educational, theological, cultural, and geographical factors suggest that middle colony Reformed clergy would have differed from their New England counterparts in political ideology. The great majority of New England ministers were educated at Harvard or Yale; while some middle colony preachers were trained at Yale, the majority were educated at the College of New Jersey, the Log College of William Tennent, or in Old World institutions. New England clerics, except in Rhode Island, were predominantly Congregationalists; the middle colony Reformed ministers were almost entirely Presbyterians, Dutch Reformed, German Reformed, or Baptists. Theologically, increasing numbers of New England ministers deviated from Calvinism or even adopted Arminian tenets, while the middle colony Reformed generally maintained classic Reformed statements of faith. Finally, the high member-to-minister ratio in the larger land areas most likely taxed the powers of even the most energetic middle colony minister, unlike the ratio in the concentrated city base of the Congregationalists.

Even though all these environmental and intellectual distinctives are considerable, there are more similarities than differences between the war ideologies of the New England and middle colony Reformed clergymen. The regionalism of the middle colony Reformed clergymen did not dominate their common theological heritage.

What was true of the state of religion in the middle colonies was true politically and ethnically also, and the reticence of the middle colonies to rebel against the authority of the British Crown may have been a reflection of the lack of a coherent political theology, of the kind which had been hammered home week after week for many decades by the Congregationalists in New England. There was no single group or class to whom the middle colony masses looked for leadership. Neither was there any identifiable group whose authority was as accepted as that of the New England pastors or the southern plantation patricians. While one might expect that the middle colony response to the New England call to insurrection would be at best uneven, within certain groups there was a unified response to the pressures being exerted by the political and military events around them.

Only after the middle colonies had been invaded did the Reformed Protestant group present a unified patriotic affirmation of armed resistance. This conservatism, followed by reluctant patriotic support of revolution, can be accounted for largely by theological considerations, at least among the middle colony Reformed clergy. Unfortunately, the work of ascertaining just what those considerations were is doubly difficult for a number of reasons.

First, though the middle colonies were less eager to revolt than either New England or the South, they were the first and worst devastated by British expeditions designed to cut off the Northeast from the South. The British, invading New Jersey and New York, destroyed much of the personal effects of the people, including libraries and sermons of the middle colony Reformed clergy. The literary productions of the latter were perceived as propaganda and catalysts to revolutionary sentiment.[3] Second, most of the sermons of the middle colony Reformed ministers dealt with salvation and the Christian life. Third, because there was no established church, there was no tradition of special occasion sermons (such as election day or fast day sermons) dealing with political topics. Fourth, there were far fewer printing presses in the middle colonies than in the cities of New England.

Lastly, the pietistic tendencies of the Dutch Reformed, German Reformed, and the Baptists in this period decreased references to temporal affairs in pulpit sermons, though their patriotic efforts equaled those of the Presbyterians. All of these factors combined make the number of extant documents from the middle colony Reformed clergy seem minuscule compared to that available from New England clerics. But enough of the political literature produced by ordained middle colony Reformed clergymen in the period of 1740 to 1763 has survived from which their resistance ideology can be reconstructed.[4]

Even though that reconstruction may be possible, the question remains, just how great of an audience would have been within reach of their sermons supporting war or revolution? Some writers' estimates of church membership in the eighteenth century are as low as ten percent of the population, while some have suggested that, even in New England, church membership was probably at best one-fifth of the population, and most likely less for the middle colonies.[5] This is actually irrelevant, though, for measuring influence because becoming a member of an eighteenth century Calvinistic church was a far more rigorous event than today, even if a congregation had been organized within traveling distance. Moreover, "adherence" or regular attendance at a local congregation ranged from eighty percent in 1700 to approximately sixty percent in 1780.[6] So perhaps one-half of the colonists were hearing the weekly (or more frequent) sermons of the middle colony clergy. Since the Reformed communions—Dutch Reformed, Presbyterians, German Reformed, and Baptists—accounted for more than half of the churches in the middle colonies,[7] and since the local minister in the period under consideration was likely to be one of the most educated, informed, and influential men in the area, the number of people being influenced by their resistance ideology amounted to one-quarter to possibly one-half of the population.

POSSIBLE MOTIVATIONS FOR REFORMED RESISTANCE

A number of motives which may lie behind the colonial clergy's acceptance of war and revolution in the mid-eighteenth century have been suggested. Carl Bridenbaugh hypothesized that in America, fear of oppression by Anglican bishops from 1689 to 1775 created the impetus to justify revolution by the clergy.[8] It may also be possible that a kind of "civil millennialism" influenced the middle colony Reformed as has been suggested for the New England clergy.[9] Alternatively, there is no doubt that seventeenth century liberal, republican political thought grandly influenced, if not dominated, the thinking of many New England ministers in the eighteenth century;[10] so, whether the middle colony Reformed simply appropriated that kind of political thought must be considered.

While all of these may have motivated the New England clergymen, the primary sources show that more basic for middle colony Reformed resistance ideology were theological concepts: God's providence and man's means, natural law, God's judgment of sin, and, in an unexpected manner, the "people of God." The first three constitute continuities with normative Reformed theology; the last, an anomalous application of historical Reformed resistance theory.

With the middle colonies bordering the Anglican establishment in Virginia to the south, and Presbyterians having fought unsuccessfully for years to gain official recognition by British administrations in New York, it might be thought that the Reformed clergy would have concerned themselves with the possibility of Episcopal oppression. But the fear of oppression before 1764 was almost exclusively fear of Roman Catholic oppressions.[11] New York Presbyterian Samuel Buell's 1746 anti-Catholic tirade had nothing but praise for the Duke of Cumberland and his providential victory over the papist pretender, Charles Edward. If the papists had won, he warned, then "thousands" of "horrid errors . . . relating to Church and State would have been introduced."[12] There was no mention by Buell of Anglican oppression such as one finds in Jonathan Mayhew's 1750 *Unlimited Submission and Non-resistance to the Higher Powers*, in which he highlighted the abuses of Laud's administration.[13]

A decade after Buell, Aaron Burr, revivalist and President of the College of New Jersey,[14] described Britain as the "bulwark of the Reformation"[15] and praised Governor Belcher as the champion of religious freedom in New Jersey.[16] In 1759, Robert Smith, an Irish-born New Sider who studied under Samuel Blair, pointed out that God's providence was very clearly at work in the removal of Queen Anne and the defeat of the pretender, thus removing "us" from the "dreaded bondage of popish tyranny."[17] Like the others, Smith foreshortened his historical horizon to exclude the Anglican persecution of Puritans in the previous century.

While the German Reformed ministers in this period were almost totally absorbed in constructing a viable ecclesiastical organization,[18] they did make sure that the British authorities perceived them as loyal subjects. In 1754, twelve of the better known German Reformed ministers, including John Conrad Steiner, Michael Schlatter, and Henry William Stoy, sent an address in Latin to the governor of Pennsylvania, Robert Morris, when he took office. Although, as with most of the letters of this kind, it consisted mostly of flattery, in it they took pains to assure Morris that what they taught would lead the Germans to "understand the duties of man as citizen and Christian." And,

> most honorable Sir, the Christian religion does indeed not loosen the bonds of society but rather strengthens them, does not disturb the body politic, but pacifies it, does not wound, but heal; in a word, piety establishes government.[19]

In 1761, even more praise and submission were offered to the British Crown by Philadelphia German Reformed preacher John Conrad Steiner. In a memorial to the death of King George II, *Schuldigstes Liebes-und Ehren-Denkmahl*, Steiner created an effusive, extended parallel of George II to Moses. Later, in the same document, he prayed that God would "fill the young monarch [George III] richly with the spirit of Moses and Joshua."[20] A greater expression of pietistic-Calvinistic submission to government could hardly have been printed, and it showed that the German Reformed in this period demonstrated as much loyalty to the British Crown as any High Church Tory.

Dutch Reformed minister and arguably the fountainhead of the Great Awakening, Theodore Frelinghuysen praised George II, "His Majesty, King George, our most gracious Sovereign, always taking tender Care of the Concerns of his liege, loyal, and loving Subjects . . . having the Interests of his Dominions in America much at heart," for having resisted the French incursions.[21]

Presbyterian revivalist and later president of the College of New Jersey, Samuel Davies displayed a similar loyalty to the British Crown. To him King George II was the champion of religious freedom *par excellence*, for the latter, Davies averred, was aware that "the imposition of uniformity in minute points of faith, or in forms of worship or ecclesiastical government" was not consistent with "rights of private judgment." This George was the guardian of Protestants in general, of "Dissenter as well as Conformist." To Davies, "liberty, the Protestant religion and George II . . . are inseparably united."[22] It would seem then that Davies perceived the king as the arbiter of religious tolerance between Anglican and dissenter. By that perception he, at least obliquely, recognized the possibility of Anglican domination even in his time. But this recognition did not in the least vitiate Davies's exhortations to the colonists to fight for Britain and themselves against France.

On the other hand, some middle colony Reformed ministers were sensitive to an Anglican menace. Old Side Presbyterian professor at the College of Philadelphia, Francis Alison, while writing to Ezra Stiles in 1759, warned that the divisions existing among Connecticut Congregationalists would bring about their being "swallowed up by the Episcopal Church, who envy their prosperity and will avail themselves of these divisions."[23] Alison's 1763 thanksgiving sermon for the Treaty of Paris also showed more historical awareness of past Anglican abuses of power, even while he thanked God for allowing him and his congregation not to have been born in a former age:

We are called to prepare for eternal life not in the dark ages of popery nor in the reign of Henry our cruel and haughty reformer nor in the reign of his bloody daughter Mary nor in the reign of Elisabeth and James where acts of uniformity and star chambers and persecutions vexed some of the best subjects in England, nor were we called into being in that turbulent period which is stained with tyranny, persecution, regicide, and civil wars when arbitrary and cruel powers were claimed and exercised by all in authority, civil and ecclesiastical.

Alison added that they lived in an era where civil and religious liberty was known and practiced, and "no man is persecuted for the rights of conscience."[24] In his public addresses, Alison feared only the Catholic hierarchy; in his perception, religious tolerance reigned in the British empire. Consequently, colonists who were members of communities which preserved civil and religious liberties were obliged to defend those communities "even at the expense of our lives."[25]

Whatever effect knowledge of former Anglican oppression or the possibility of future dominance by the Episcopal hierarchy may have had upon the provincial politics of the period, or on the ties to dissenting groups in England,[26] that knowledge did not diminish calls by mid-century middle colony Reformed clergy to take up arms in defense of British colonial lives, property, and the Protestant religion against the French "papists." The middle colony Reformed thoroughly identified themselves and their constituents with the British, even with cultural diversity surrounding them. Fear of episcopacy was unrelated to the development of middle colony Reformed ideology. Rather, the fear of bishops was specifically the fear of Catholic bishops, and in this, the middle colony clergy were like the seventeenth century Puritans who feared Catholicism more than any other temporal power.

While Bridenbaugh labored to demonstrate that it was the fear of Episcopal oppression that motivated colonial ministers to finally justify armed conflict with the British, Nathan Hatch put forth another, very different hypothesis concerning their motivations. Hatch denies that there is a direct and major connection between the values of the Great Awakening and the fueling of the Revolutionary War, for he perceives in the intervening period of imperial wars a significant transformation of traditional New England apocalyptic eschatology. New England Old and New Lights, after the loss of revival fervency, identified the French defeats in America with the Antichrist and his last days' defeat. Hatch concludes that "in this new eschatology the French were identified with cosmic evil as much for their civil tyranny as for any other reason."[27]

While these clergymen idealized British civil and religious liberties, the middle colony Reformed clergymen also saw the imperial wars religiously, as part of the Protestant struggle against the papal Antichrist. For example, Buell identifies Bonnie Prince Charlie as the "grandson" of Beelzebub, and a tyrannical papist.[28] Revivalist Gilbert Tennent interpreted the war as, in reality, a spiritual conflict: "Satan excites, and [the] Antichrist carries on, against the Church of God, for their inviolable adherence to divine truths."[29] Yale graduate Ebenezer Prime possessed no certainty about the war and its relationship to the millennium:

> it is difficult, perhaps impossible to determine . . . when this grand event shall take place, still more . . . what shall be the issue of particular struggles between the protestant and antichristian forces . . . what will be the event of the present war with our popish enemies . . .[30]

Samuel Davies had no more certainty about the issue of the war.[31]

Robert Smith believed that "presently" the Antichrist would be destroyed; for him, the millennium was that period in which Islam's "delusion," Jewish "infidelity," and pagan "idolatry" would all be annihilated. The gospel would be spread across the earth, and the church militant would reign in glory.[32] The conservative Alison was making no conflation of civil and religious millennial hopes when he wrote, "popery has gotten the mortal blow in North America, and there is . . . unexpected prospect that the protestant religion will extend to the north pole. . . . All the revolutions . . . have been so ordered by him as to promote the grand design of restoring mankind and to advance that Kingdom of Righteousness."[33]

The Dutch Reformed Theodore Frelinghuysen, who held to the ancient seven thousand year scheme of eschatology, also excoriated the French for their military-political treachery, and cried, "We must then either die, or submit to Servitude and Tyranny, to Idolatry, Superstition, and Thraldom." However, Frelinghuysen was simply following the well-trod path of his Calvinistic forebears in seeing an indissoluble connection between religious and political freedom, rather than any civil millennialism, for in his eschatology there was another 250 years after his lifetime before "the glorious State of the Church"— i.e., the millennium—came.[34]

Although in the above sermons the French were identified as papist instruments of the Antichrist, no clear identification of biblical apocalyptic events with current political events presented itself. Beam's conclusion that the emerging millennialism of the middle colony Presbyterians was an "elaboration of the traditional belief that the churches of New England had a special mission to redeem the world"[35] is a more accurate comprehension than either Hatch's or Bridenbaugh's. On the other hand, even he misses the incongruity of *middle colony* Reformed clergy preaching that message in their pluralistic environment.[36]

What is indicated in the Reformed vision of the kingdom of God spreading across America is the bud of a religious Manifest Destiny ideology. Inasmuch as the Roman Catholic French appeared as the great obstacle to expansion of the kingdom westward, they had to be combatted. The anti-Catholicism of the colonial Reformed clergy is but one strand of continuity present in their resistance ideology, clearly inherited from the British Puritan tradition, and the continental Reformed tradition before it. Also inherited from those latter traditions, and used as justification for war against the French, is natural law and the complex of ideas historically associated with it.

NATURAL LAW AND SOCIAL COMPACT CONTINUITIES

Natural law and the social compact theory of government have been seen as having a decisive influence on the New England patriot preachers in the pre-Revolutionary period.[37] Natural law was a fundamental part of the political ideology of the middle colony Reformed clergy, also. Samuel Davies in 1756 paralleled natural law and revelation when he wrote that natural law or reason taught the pagan, while revelation instructed the Christian.[38] Later, in 1758, he mentioned in passing that the idea that sins cause national calamities was a law essential to both natural and revealed religion.[39] Log College graduate and later president of the College of New Jersey, Samuel Finley, in his sermon on Judges 5:23, appealed to the principle of the "natural equity" of self-defense, for it was the "original law." The pacifists, he declared, twist "every text . . . contrary to the eternal reason of things and many other Scriptures."[40] While expositing the meaning of Christian meekness and affirming Christian community resistance to violation of rights, Old Sider John Ewing, Alison's protégé and colleague, appealed to the regulation of passions by reason and religion.[41]

Frelinghuysen deemed defensive wars "both lawful and our indispensible Duty," on the bases of Scripture, history, and "the Nature of Things." Self-defense was valid because the "Principle of Self-preservation" was "implanted in human Nature," so that, analogous to the individual that defends himself from a robber, nations should also defend themselves against unwarranted aggression.[42]

But the greatest use of natural reason in relation to politics and revolution is made, perhaps unexpectedly, by Gilbert Tennent, son of the founder of the Log College. Tennent held that the dictates of reason were equivalent to the law of nature. Self-defense, Tennent preached, "the clearest reason dictates, and the tenderest passion recommends; it is a principle so deeply riveted in human nature that it is unnatural to doubt of its lawfulness."[43] Moral precepts were grounded upon the "nature and reason of things" and upon "invariable equity" and therefore could not be altered. Jesus came not to destroy either the "moral law or the law of nature," rather "the Light of nature, the law of God, and the gospel of Christ" all confirmed the validity of a defensive war.[44]

While the degree to which these staunch Calvinists cite reason or natural law may seem striking, it should be observed that natural reason did not take first place in their considerations, nor was there a transmutation of Scriptural arguments into natural reason and dictates of conscience as in the deistic thinkers of that period. Rather, given the historical Reformed perspective on natural law as found, distilled in the moral law of the Scriptures, it would be entirely consistent with the whole Reformed tradition to validate defensive war on the basis of "the nature of things" or natural law. Appeals to the natural law of self-defense came to the fore when dealing with government and political issues.[45] Intimately connected with the eighteenth century ideas of government, natural law, and self-defense was the concept of the social compact, which also appears in the middle colony resistance sermons.

James McAllister has persuasively argued that both Francis Alison and John Witherspoon theorized that the social compact established the foundation for government. By analyzing the lecture notebooks of one of Alison's students from 1759, McAllister demonstrates Alison's strong dependence upon Scottish philosopher Francis Hutcheson, whose complete system of moral philosophy was published in London in 1755. Hence, a direct influence of English Republican thought can be traced down to middle colony Reformed ministers from Harrington to Hutcheson through the latter's student Alison.[46] And of course, a version of the compact is found in Witherspoon's lectures on moral philosophy, though it is impossible to say now which part of those lectures was delivered prior to the Revolution.

Nonetheless, it is not necessary to look to either Alison or one of his students for evidence that the idea of the social compact was used by the middle colony Reformed clergy. For example, Gilbert Tennent, in one of his longest published sermons during the French and Indian War, asked,

> What is Civil Government but the Union of Individuals, for the more effectual Protection of Person and Property from Injustice and Violence? . . . whereby a sufficient Measure of Power is, by common Consent, treasured up for the Security and Benefit of all the Members of that Body, which is to be exerted to compass the afore said important Ends.[47]

Samuel Davies, when lamenting the death of George II, said that the British constitution was "but the voluntary compact of sovereign and subject."

Conversely, there is scant evidence that the middle colony Reformed went straight to John Locke in using the social compact as the real foundation of government. In another place, when urging fathers to institute "family religion," Davies seems to indicate that government naturally grew out of the family; but he also observes, as did other middle colony Reformed preachers, that without government "liberty and property could not be secured . . . men would turn savages and roam at large, destitute of religion, insensible of the human passions, and regardless of human welfare."[48] This kind of preaching suggests that, even if some version of the social compact is found in the thought of the middle colony Reformed clergy, it is not a pure Lockean kind of compact; the Reformed doctrine of depravity may have overshadowed Locke's idyllic state of nature.

MAGISTRACY AND JUST WARS: MORE CONTINUITY

The patriotic Reformed clergy during the imperial war years made more use of their view of the magistracy than of the social compact. In calling the local government officials to account, Gilbert Tennent warned that if colonists on the frontier were "wronged and robbed of their just right" by magistrates delaying justice and protection by the sword, then those magistrates were guilty of destroying the very *raison d'être* of their office, which would then become "a mere cypher, of no moment and consequence to society."[49] Tennent evidently had in mind implicating the Quaker-dominated government of Pennsylvania. Such a charge was not just a politically motivated rhetorical device; rather, to the Reformed mind, protection by the magistrates' swords was a normal function of government. For example, in a sermon "preached upon the public execution of one Hugh Gillespie" the Reverend Chauncy Graham of the Dutchess County Presbytery, charged the attending government officials:

> You are ministers of God, for the good of his people . . . the executive power of penal laws is put into your hands; You wear the sword of civil justice, which is the sword of the Lord; let it not rust in the scabbard or be worn in vain, but ever keep it drawn in the cause of God and the public.[50]

To the eighteenth century middle colony Reformed clergy, the magistrate was to use force to enforce God's will on society, whether dispensing penal justice to felons, or invoking the natural law of self-defense when his subjects were attacked by foreign armies.

If the magistrate was charged with defense of the country from foreign invaders, he was still bound to carry out only a just war in reaction. As previously discussed, the Reformed tradition made the magistrate the central agent in its just war ideology, and it was especially within the Puritan branch of Reformed Protestantism that just war theory was developed. The middle colony Reformed clergy appropriated that tradition and rigorously applied it to their situation.

For these Reformed clergy, God would bless only just wars with success, and only defensive wars were just. The imperial wars in America were defensive, and therefore just. The British colonies had been invaded and their resources taken, and this made the invading French robbers. Even allowing for wartime exaggeration, Ebenezer Prime must have inflated his numbers when he declared, "our lands have been invaded, properties and possessions taken by unrighteousness encroachments and many thousands of our fellow subjects barbarously murdered by French papists and their cruel subjects."[51] Samuel Finley averred that it was "well-known, that the French had seized on the

Lands of Ohio, and were fortifying themselves within the British Territories, before a Sword was drawn against them." Moreover, these outrages were perpetrated in violation of "former treaties" which "have been produced, that shew, the French were circumscribed in such Bounds as do not reach near the Ohio."[52] Therefore, the enemy were considered covenant breakers as well as thieves. Since the French had violated the Decalogue's laws against lying, stealing, and killing, the magistrates of the colonies were well justified in warring against them.

Furthermore, not only were these natural laws broken by the papists, but the middle colony Reformed clergy perceived that the "pure religion of Jesus, streaming uncorrupted from the sacred fountain of the Scriptures" *would* be destroyed if the tyrannical Catholics were to conquer.[53] The middle colony Reformed clergy based this kind of prediction primarily on the historical experience of the Huguenots, but some also added the trials of mid-eighteenth century French Reformed victims. Often the middle colony Reformed clergy added that war was undertaken only as a "last resort" to show that the enemy was indeed implacable.

Gilbert Tennent most fully exposited the criteria by which a war was deemed just. A defensive war was just when it was carried according to the following criteria: for protection of personal or property rights; for the recovery of something taken of which the consequences of doing without were more "distressing" than those of war; by the magistrate for the punishment of great injury which affected the credit or interest of a collective of people; and when it probably would be successful.[54] In arguing for Christians to engage in a just war, Tennent sharply distinguished those offenses committed against personal rights from those against national rights. John Ewing, when considering the pacifistic injunctions contained in the Sermon on the Mount, made the same distinction.[55] Christian responses to personal and national injuries were to differ; for both Ewing and Tennent, war was permitted for national injuries. But even when explaining the Sermon on the Mount, Ewing argued against allowing others to destroy an individual's "natural rights" without resisting them. That kind of pacifistic response not only would be un-Christian, but it actually would subvert society and civil government. Peace could not be preserved at the expense of conscience, innocence, or truth. To give away the right of private judgment or to submit to human inventions in religion—i.e., Catholicism—would be to court divine displeasure,[56] an echo of Knox's sixteenth century admonition to rout out idolatry as part of a national covenant.

Divine displeasure in response to the sins of the colonists dominated the middle colony Reformed jeremiads, and the theological doctrine which explained that displeasure was God's providence. John Berens has shown that this doctrine pervaded all eighteenth century American thought,[57] but the middle colony Reformed clergy perceived that doctrine being particularly and acutely worked out in their colonies during the imperial wars.

GOD'S ACTS AMONG THE NATIONS

To the middle colony Reformed ministers God was the moral governor of the world and of all history. He operated directly on moral agents as instruments of His will, on unbelievers as well as His chosen people. In particular, the Lord intervened on behalf of specific armies in response to the prayers of the godly. Yale graduate Abraham Keteltas cited not only Scripture to prove this point, but also past and contemporary historical events.[58] In order to uphold His honor and His moral government, God had to chastise His chosen people, even if He did this to benefit them, to draw them back to Himself, preventing their condemnation with the world, according to George Duffield.[59] Chastisements frequently came from not only nature but also godless human rods of judgment. In the Old Testament those rods were Assyria and Babylon; in the New Testament it was Rome. For the colonies in this period, the rods were France and the Indians.[60]

Just as the middle colony Reformed clergy distinguished between offenses against individuals and nations when discussing the just war, so also they dichotomized God's judgments and rewards between individuals and nations. Though individuals might receive rewards or chastisements in this life or the next, nations were judged in this world alone, for they would not exist in the next.[61] Judgments for nations, as well as individuals, came in recompense for specific sins: blessings were given to the righteous. Since personal sins hindered corporate war efforts, nearly all the wartime sermons included calls for personal repentance and reformation. The colonists had not repented in consequence of the first French and Indian War (1740–48); so, they declared, "heavier strokes have fell on us."[62] In these jeremiads, the preachers inevitably called for a repentance to cleanse the land but, notably for this point in time, both Britain and her colonists were included as the sufferers of judgments, as well as the sinners whose sins provoked those judgments.[63]

Throughout these declarations of God's providential workings, the concept of means reappeared. God brought "his purposes to pass by a chain of subordinate causes,"[64] or by means of men; e.g., for Buell, the Duke of Cumberland, for Alison, William Pitt the Elder. Since, Prime asserted, there were no more miracles as in the Old Testament to guide and protect the saints, Christians had to be "up and doing" to acquire skill in warfare.[65] On the other hand, God's people at war still needed prayer and reformation of moral life: they had to depend upon God to achieve the blessing of victory. Samuel Finley was not so dogmatic: God might work miracles by choice, but to limit

Him to them would be a "most daring presumption."[66] For the Reformed clergy of the middle colonies, the magistrate served as the focal means by which God would work out His will for political society; this conception of governmental officials had already been well developed in their theological ancestors Calvin and the later Puritan theologians.[67] Seeing government in this way again confirms the indebtedness of the middle colony Reformed clergy to their religious heritage.

While most of the middle colony Reformed ministers stressed the role of means when exhorting their listeners to prepare for war, Duffield discerned another, more spiritual, function for means within the providential framework. God, he said, allowed afflictions to come to His people so that they might see the insufficiency of all means without His gracious assistance. For God to accomplish something, whether with or without means, when human efforts seem baffled was all the more divine and brought more glory to Himself.[68]

Regardless of how much emphasis an individual preacher might put on either God's gracious interventions or the need for appropriate means, still the middle colony Reformed providential perspective was optimistic. During the war Samuel Davies thought that the outcome was "dismally uncertain." But after discussing the books of Revelation and Daniel, he saw that *if* that war was the "commencement of this great decisive conflict between the Lamb and the Beast," then it would signal the beginning of the "most glorious and happy revolution the world would ever see." And although "all other empires and kingdoms of the world have been subject to revolutions, passed from hand to hand, and at length fallen to pieces" and even though "we and millions more should be crushed in the grand revolution," yet that finally established kingdom would be eternal.[69] Alison, as mentioned before, after the 1763 peace treaty had been signed, preached in glowing terms that all wars were furthering God's "grand design."[70]

"GOD'S COVENANT PROTESTANT PEOPLE"

While the doctrines of natural law, the function of the magistrate, providence, means, and God's judgments in history represent continuities which the Reformed ministers of the middle colonies adopted from the sixteenth century Puritan tradition, their use of the concept of the "people of God" presents an unusual adaptation of the doctrine of the church. Its application to the pluralistic middle colonies is unexpected, and may be a distortion brought about by the urgency to mobilize colonial armed forces in response to external threat.

God's people, it seems, were all the people listening to or reading these sermons. This extension of the concept of the church appears to stand behind all their political sermons of the war years, even though it contradicts the calls for conversion within the messages themselves. It also contradicts the reality of the social environment in which they delivered these messages: i.e., communities filled with, at best, nominal Christians, as well as those the middle colony Reformed clergy perceived as heretics, e.g., Quakers. The whole society was labeled the people of God, in opposition to the Catholics, whether they were the French in the current war, English Jacobins in the recent past, or Mary I (Bloody Mary) in the remote past.

For a sermon to be published indicates that it was deemed important for more ears than just those of merely a single congregation. Of course, publication might have just been the end result of an influential patron's whim and a preacher's pride. Fortunately, eighteenth century pamphlets and tracts often give the circumstances of delivery and/or publication, or at least indicate by their dedications that the piece was published with the greater community in mind.

The sermons examined in this chapter were given in sundry circumstances. As noted above, Graham's published sermon *God Will Trouble the Troublers of His People* was given on the day of the execution of a felon, which at that time was still a public event that even children attended. This information and the sermon's contents—that sinners, having caused God's wrath to fall on the whole believing community, should be penalized by just and godly magistrates—demonstrate that the preacher extended the concept of the people of God to the whole community. Two of Samuel Davies's sermons, *The Curse of Cowardice* and *Religion and Patriotism*, were not only originally preached to companies of volunteer provincial militia, but were also reprinted in New York, New Jersey, Boston, and Philadelphia. His *The Crisis*, preached on a general fast day in Virginia, was also reprinted in Philadelphia, as was his *On the Death of His Late Majesty, King George II*. Davies's *Religion and Public Spirit* was originally delivered at the College of New Jersey before being printed in Philadelphia. Abraham Keteltas's *The Religious Soldier* was "preached . . . to the regular officers and soldiers in Elizabethtown" in New York.[71]

Probably the most diverse audience specified in these published sermons was that given by Ebenezer Prime's *The Importance of the Divine Presence*, which was preached "to the provincials . . . at Long Island" and "published in compliance with the desires of a number of the soldiers, inhabitants and strangers that were hearers."[72] Though Samuel Finley proposed with his popular and acerbic *Curse of Meroz* "to cast my mite into the public treasury," he modestly admits that it was "preached at desire of many" in order "to engage the attention of mankind."[73] The two addresses by Aaron Burr were originally delivered at public ceremonies as befitted his role of president of the College of New Jersey. He preached "a funeral sermon . . . at the interment of his late excellency Jonathan Belcher, Esq., governor of his majesty's province," and the "substance of what is here offered to the public," was delivered on a "day set apart for solemn fasting and prayer."[74]

Even in those messages in which the original audience was undetermined or limited to a single congregation, the dedications to public figures or groups in the publication prefaces indicate that, at least in published form, the message was intended for the pluralistic middle colony public. For example, those sermons by New Siders Joseph Treat and Gilbert Tennent, though perhaps preached to their home congregations, were dedicated respectively to the captain general and governor-in-chief of the province of New York, and the provincial and city magistrates of Philadelphia, along with the 600-member Association for Defense in that city.

Thus, there is a strong probability that, once published, the sermons above were intended for the general public.[75] The general public would have included those outside denominational boundaries, and so it could be said that these Reformed ministers did, in practice if not formal doctrine, extend the concept of the people of God to the whole community.

While the Presbyterians of this period accepted the traditional Reformed distinction between the visible and invisible church,[76] they accentuated the Church Universal, in contrast to the New England Congregationalists. But even with a very strong sense of the Church Universal, to include within the church the whole community constitutes a quantum leap. Even if it could be argued that the Great Awakening blurred both class distinctions and denominational borders, producing a popular sense of intercolonial unity, yet the Awakening also split the Reformed denominations into acrimoniously warring factions that remained hostile well into the 1760s.

No justification was given for these extensions of the church. Though these sermons were hortatory addresses to congregations and the general communities under the tensions of war, it is notable that these preachers made no mention of a role for the church as distinct from society in general. There was no distinction made between unconverted ministers or their followers and true believers—a highly divisive issue in the Great Awakening. Rather, the American colonists to whom these messages were delivered were designated simplistically as God's people. More instructive than a mere psychological-sociological interpretation of this phenomenon would be an examination of the historical theological heritage of these Reformed ministers.

Probably envisioned in the minds of these Reformed ministers was the kind of society delineated by the seventeenth century Puritans, and the fifteenth century Reformers, especially John Knox.[77] In covenant with God and each other, both rulers and ruled alike in that kind of commonwealth were accountable to their Lord, regardless of denominational differences. In such a social arrangement, church and society would not be sharply distinguished, but rather would function together, ministering the two swords to the same people, and from behind closed ranks, the sword of war to invaders, especially to Catholics. This commonwealth is the kind of organic, integrated society presupposed by the texts of the Old Testament brought out to support the ethics of warfare by the middle colony Reformed.

The Christian commonwealth model also formed the backdrop for the claims asserted by Samuel Davies when he proclaimed that God is the God of America,[78] and by Ebenezer Prime when he explicitly paralleled the middle colonies with Israel in the Conquest.[79] Their extension of the concept of the "people of God" to the whole pluralistic community of the middle colonies can be clarified by considering the many historical allusions in their works. Certainly, the pilgrim myth of the New England fathers was strong in the mind of Aaron Burr, when he wistfully referred to the "spirit of our brave ancestors . . . in a howling wilderness."[80] Francis Alison must have been thinking along the same lines when he declared, "We are called to live to God . . . in this wilderness," while preaching in urbane Philadelphia in 1763.[81] Davies excoriated "our country" for having "sinned on securely for above one hundred and fifty years," while "exposed in this savage wilderness."[82] Finley warned his hearers of the failure to transmit their heritage of liberty, property, and religion which they received from "our fathers" who "purchased this goodly heritage for us for the price of great labour and much blood."[83]

Unexpectedly, even the ethnic Dutch Frelinghuysen identifies himself with his audience from New England, when he refers to "our venerable and pious Ancestors," who for the sake of religious freedom, immigrated to America when it "was nothing else than a vast Desart, and an howling Wilderness."[84] Perhaps the most suggestive expression indicating how the middle colony Reformed perceived the role of the American colonists in God's economy might be Ebenezer Prime's designation of them as: "God's covenant protestant people."[85] This phrase liberally allowed the inclusion of those with whom the middle colony Reformed did not agree theologically, while conveniently excluding the Catholics. In this way, all Protestants could be joined together under this umbrella term, and the Catholics held apart as the enemy.

The Reformed clergy reinforced this simplistic polarization of middle colony society into Protestants and Catholics by hearkening back for their identity to Protestant victories over Catholics in early seventeenth and eighteenth century Britain. Davies groaned to think about "what would have been our situation under the . . . name of Stuart." He also rejoiced that the "despicable pretender"—which Buell had anathematized fifteen years earlier—was subdued under King George II.[86] Robert Smith not only cited deliverance from the pretender, but reached back to appropriate for their heritage the death of Queen Anne, the Gunpowder Plot, and the destruction of the Spanish Armada, as did Alison in his 1763 paean for the peace treaty.[87]

The extension of the people of God concept to the whole community must be striking to the historian of the middle colonies, for not only were the communicants of the Reformed churches never a majority of the population, but the legal restrictions placed upon them must have in some sense put them outside the ruling classes. Of the total number of Protestant congregations in the middle colonies, the Presbyterians accounted for only 187 of the 590 existing in 1750, approximately thirty-one percent.[88] As noted before, Presbyterians never achieved legal status in New York in this period. In Pennsylvania, though, the Presbyterians enjoyed that province's religious tolerance along with many sects; the Quakers—whom the Reformed looked upon as theological miscreants—retained control of the government. Nonpolitical Reformed sermons of this mid-century period attacked Quakers, Moravians, and German pietists as heretics or worse.

The Reformed social ethic of this period helps to explain why they were able to include many under the label of "God's protestant covenant people." They elevated the community and "public spirit" to such a level that their ethics might have been skewed. For example, John Ewing interpreted Matthew 5:5 to mean that Christians are to "bear lesser injuries . . . as far as is consistent with our obligation to promote the welfare of the community."[89] On the other side of the Presbyterian fold, Gilbert Tennent urged his hearers to have regard for the "whole community, of which we are a part" and "to promote its interests, in the most diffusive manner we are capable of!"[90] To Samuel Davies, King David was worthy of imitation because he combined within himself "two things, public spirit and religion." This combination produced "a proper member of human society, and even of the grand community of angels and saints." Indeed, Davies even declaims, "And so inseparably are these [public spirit and religion] united, that the one cannot exist in the entire absence of the other."[91]

Alan Heimert appears to have been right in his analysis of the importance of the social theory of the eighteenth century Calvinists,[92] but he fails to see that Old Siders as well as New Siders supported the same kind of communitarian perspective. This elevation of the community might be seen as simply a device to motivate those whom they knew would not be convinced by direct biblical or philosophical arguments. But to Samuel Davies, especially influential because of his position as president of the College of New Jersey, elevation of the community was a logical working out of the Christian life of "equity" towards those living around the believer; e.g., so that the Gospel might be well received. Social obligations were a very weighty matter, directly related to salvation:

> I shall only add, that unless you conscientiously observe the duties of social life, you cannot enter the kingdom of heaven. Not only sins done immediately against God, the omission of duties to him, but also sins against our fellow-

creatures, and the omission of the duties we owe to them, will exclude men from the kingdom of God.[93]

Gilbert Tennent concurred, saying that to look to private interests ahead of the commonweal "betrays a narrow, a groveling, a mean, a sneaking, a sordid mind."[94] Such a social ethic, integrated into a potentially legalistic predestinarian Reformed theology, matched the rigor of any previous perspective on the public Christian life. This kind of Reformed religion would certainly have functioned as a unifying, energizing force in mobilizing a society at war.

This chapter has evinced the difficulty of assuming that the middle colony Reformed clergy preached a political ideology with the same content as that of the New England ministers; it has shown that the middle colony Reformed were truly heirs of the earlier Puritan political tradition, especially as it related to armed combat. For example, the fear of Anglican domination was almost irrelevant in this period. Moreover, there was no well-developed civil millennialism for the middle colony Reformed.[95] Like the seventeenth century Puritans, though, the middle colony Reformed clergy did justify the taking up of arms in a just, defensive war. They did hold on to the use of natural—i.e., moral—law, in their justifications. Following the Puritans, they held the magistrate accountable to be the principal agent in just war actions. Furthermore, they saw God at work in history, providentially moving nations and peoples, especially His elect, and dispensing judgments and rewards through secondary instruments. These doctrines form continuities with Reformed thought; assuming the whole middle colony community as the people of God creates a distinct discontinuity.

These war sermons were designed to move whole, pluralistic communities against a common threat. Thus denominational distinctives were ignored. A dominant identification with the English-speaking, British Isles Puritan tradition extended the life of the Christian commonwealth social model already formulated in sixteenth and seventeenth century British and Scottish Reformed thought. That social theory held the entire community liable to God's judgment for sin, for the whole community was in covenant with God. The pluralism of the middle colonies necessitated some kind of Christian commonwealth idea by the middle colony preachers if they were to move enough troops into the battlefield to save God's covenant Protestant people from the Antichrist and his instruments.

The traditional, Reformed reliance on the Old Testament furnished the hermeneutical infrastructure for this Reformed war ideology and the social theory behind it. Without that hermeneutic, their war ideology could not have been constructed. The concept of the covenant community underlay such passages as Jeremiah 48:10 and Judges 5:23, as well as the whole Old Testament. Indeed, they relied on the Old Testament for all their ideas about ethics wherever the New Testament did not address particular issues.

The communitarian presuppositions integral to the texts which they preached to mobilize the middle colonies could not but help shape their war ideology, and later, a justification of revolution. The expansion of the concept of "God's covenant protestant people" in this period developed in the mind of the Reformed community a sense of being a part of a greater geo-political entity; it was developing a religious nationalism. The students of these ministers, that is, the preachers and theologians of the next four decades, continued to develop the idea of "God's covenant protestant people," issuing eventually in support of the American Revolution.

4

Earlier English Political Traditions

The ideas of the early eighteenth century British commonwealthmen, such as John Trenchard, Thomas Gordon, Robert Molesworth, and Bishop Benjamin Hoadly, significantly influenced politics not only in England, but also in New England.[1] On the other hand, it is open to question whether they had any direct influence on the ethics of war and revolution taught by the middle colony Reformed clergy in the period of 1764 to 1780. By comparing the ideas found in selected works of John Milton, John Locke, and Algernon Sidney with middle colony political ethics, a considerable correspondence can be seen between the latter and the ideas of those seventeenth century English political theorists.

The earlier English resistance ideologues argued their positions partially on the basis of the whole historical tradition of the "rights of Englishmen." The middle colony Reformed clergy were also motivated to support revolution by an historical consciousness as inheritors of the British constitutional rights tradition which, in their eyes, reached its highest achievement under the early House of Hanover.

AVAILABILITY OF SECULAR POLITICAL WORKS

The educated patriots of the Revolutionary period knew well the works of the seventeenth century political writers. The political writings of Locke, Milton, Sidney, and Hoadly were widely found prior to the American Revolution in personal and lending libraries, book sale notices, and college holdings.[2] Various public figures, including the founding fathers, credit these writings as strongly influencing their own political philosophies.[3] New England patriotic clergy, as well, credit them as principal sources for their political ideas, at times citing them by name in their revolutionary sermons.[4]

It is all the more striking, therefore, that in the messages of the middle colony Reformed clergy of the period (1764–80), Locke was never cited or alluded to.[5] Though Locke, writing on government, was a "standard author" at the College of Philadelphia in the 1750s, along with Grotius, Pufendorf, and Hutcheson,[6] he may not have been, at least in the middle colonies, the central philosopher that our century has made him. In these same middle colony political sermons, as with Locke's works, there is no direct mention of Milton.[7] No citation to Sidney's works appears in the middle colony Reformed messages, although they were, along with Locke and others, on the recommended reading list for upperclassmen at the College of Philadelphia.[8] Suffering the same fate as Sidney's *Discourses*, the political output of Bishop Benjamin Hoadly is almost unknown today, even though, in the first decades of the eighteenth century, he was known as a notorious Whig for his attacks upon a resilient Tory faction in Britain.[9]

Among the middle colony Reformed, there is no hint that Hoadly was even known. There is no citation of his works, neither is there any record of them in the College of New Jersey Library up to 1760.[10] Even Professor Witherspoon, fresh from the British Isles in 1768, shows no knowledge of Hoadly in his *Lectures on Moral Philosophy*, and none, also, of the well-known commonwealthmen Trenchard or Gordon.[11] Perhaps with his knowledge of the classics and seventeenth century writers such as Locke, Samuel Rutherford, Grotius, and others, Witherspoon felt no need for using the works of the Anglican bishop. Witherspoon recommended during the years he lectured on moral philosophy the works of Locke, Grotius, Pufendorf, Harrington, Sidney, Burlamaqui, and Montesquieu.[12] However, the influence of a reading list becomes suspect when we find the Reverend Andrew Hunter, who graduated four years after Witherspoon assumed the presidency of the College of New Jersey, recording in his war diary while a chaplain with the continental troops in 1779 that he did not *begin* to read Burlamaqui until August of 1779;[13] thus, it may be safely assumed that, as with the students of today, so it was with the eighteenth century student: not all books on recommended lists were read.

Therefore, it appears that the writings of seventeenth and eighteenth century political theorists and commonwealthmen were available and used not only by the founding fathers, but also by patriotic New England clergy. No hard evidence exists, though, that the middle colony Reformed clergy had incorporated the works of English commonwealthmen in their preaching of revolution. Stray comments like Reverend Hunter's suggest that political authors like Burlamaqui were not all that well known, or at least widely read.

EFFECTS OF REGIONALISM

One possible explanation for the lack of citations of political authors is that the documents examined herein were produced mostly by Presbyterians associated with the College of New Jersey, who borrowed the preaching style of the revivalists. Such a rhetorical style denigrated authorities, used appeals directed to the personal judgment of their middle colony audience, and stood in opposition to "a paternalistic social ethic," according to Harry Stout.[14] Since the religious situation in the middle colonies was definitely weighted against "authority" in general, the various sects took every advantage to woo away parishioners from the confessional churches.[15] To counteract that kind of pressure, the middle colony Reformed clergy may have developed rhetoric free from appeals to or citations of intellectual authorities, creeds, or denominational loyalties. If this suggestion is valid, it would explain the absence of name-dropping or direct quotation of standard political works. But, even if the sermons and tracts of the middle colony Reformed clergy prove no direct dependence on classical Republicans, yet the ideas in those sermons may indicate some influence by them.

When word of the repeal of the Stamp Act reached New York in April 1766, a wave of rejoicing covered the colonies. Even the Presbyterian Synod—normally near dumb concerning political developments—published a pastoral letter in May reiterating that joy. For the next seven years, the middle colony Reformed clergy remained relatively silent on political affairs, even though the same time that the Stamp Act was repealed, the Declaratory Act was passed. This latter Act declared that the Parliament and the Crown had the right to "bind the colonies and people of America . . . in all cases whatsoever."[16] Even the politically astute Francis Alison, Old Side leader and professor at the College of Philadelphia, who in his correspondence with Ezra Stiles frequently referred to church-state matters, failed at that time to take notice of that Act. Apparently, political affairs had to reach a critical stage before the middle colony ministers perceived the breadth of that Act; only then did they repeatedly cite the Declaratory Act as the epitome of British tyranny.[17]

Two reasons may be suggested for the silence of the middle colony Reformed in the period between the repeal of the Stamp Act and the Boston Tea Party. First, New England bore the brunt of the Intolerable Acts and not the middle colonies; neither the lives nor property of the latter were being threatened. Second, as a general policy, the Reformed clergy in the middle colonies assiduously avoided making specific political pronouncements as denominations, except to petition for religious liberty.[18] Regardless of the possible reasons, these ministers were not merely dissimulating. They truly did not wish to engage in politics unless dire necessity moved them to do so. John

Adams, when commenting on a sermon by patriotic George Duffield in 1775, told his wife, "by this you will see that the clergy this way are *but now* beginning to engage in politics, and they engage with a fervor that will produce wonderful effects."[19]

On the other hand, not all the middle colony Reformed preachers were as fervently animated as the one that Adams had heard. After Lexington and Concord, Presbyterians Robert Cooper and William Foster and Baptist David Jones strenuously protested that the colonists were not seeking an independent nation status. Jones, though, added that that might "possibly be the event, but surely against our wills."[20] A number of times, in the period of 1774 to 1776 Reformed ministers and associations explicitly asserted their fealty to King George, "but," qualified John Carmichael, "we never swore allegiance to the Parliament of Great Britain—or else we would have above 500 Kings!"[21] By 1779, the Revolution was accounted, even by conservative Old Sider Matthew Wilson as "glorious struggles for liberty and independency."[22]

Although the Reformed clergy began the second half of the 1770s protesting their fealty, eventually they realized that they had to be prepared to take up arms in defense of their natural rights.[23] But, even if it were true that the "key concepts—natural rights, the contractual basis of society and government, the uniqueness of England's liberty—preserving 'mixed' constitution—were commonplaces of the liberal thought of the time,"[24] it remains to be seen which concepts were used by the middle colony clergy to justify revolution and how those concepts may have been affected by their regionalism.

NATURAL LAW

One of the commonplace concepts undergoing secularization in the mid-eighteenth century was natural law. The turning point in the *broader* history of natural law, from a metaphysical or divine law to a theory of natural rights based on autonomous human nature, is found in the writings of Grotius and Pufendorf.[25] The loss of a theistic, or biblical, perspective in the Reformed tradition in New England can be seen beginning especially in the writings of John Wise, and was carried forward into non-Reformed Congregationalism by such men as Jonathan Mayhew and Charles Chauncy. In contrast, the middle colony Reformed clergy maintained the traditional theistic foundation for natural law, which was frequently used by them to justify revolution, as will be discussed later.

A frequent difficulty for eighteenth century studies of natural law occurs because both secular and clerical figures use the same terminology with, at times, differing definitions in mind. John Locke indicated that his perspective on natural law issued from and maintained its theistic base.[26] Sidney did not deal precisely with innate ideas implanted by God, or natural law as the law of God, but rather argued from commonsense observations for the validity of the "principle of liberty in which God created us," or our "natural liberty."[27] Since Sidney's discourse is more "about the necessity of changing or overthrowing government than about government in a peaceful age,"[28] he never precisely defined natural law, but did declare that "reason, which is good inasmuch as it is from God," is a sufficient authority for argumentation.[29] Natural reason, natural law, and natural rights were all of a piece in Sidney's discourses.

Milton, the poetic genius driven by Puritan motivations, based almost his entire political theory on natural law, set firmly within a traditional Christian view of it; notably, he also said that his political system, "though it cannot but stand with plain reason, shall be made good also by Scripture."[30] This latter position is, in broad strokes, the same position taken by Puritan clergymen on both sides of the Atlantic in this period, and by the middle colony Reformed clergy in the eighteenth century. These earlier English Republican writers, living in an age that accepted, for the most part, a theistic worldview, probably did not feel compelled to make fine distinctions concerning natural law.

SOCIAL COMPACT

The middle colony Reformed clergy in the period of 1763 to 1782 apparently accepted the idea of the social compact as a basic truth about society. For example, Dutch Reformed domine Jacob R. Hardenberg, in the commencement address at Queen's College in 1774, stated, "It is manifest that Societies are formed by mutual Compacts." It is difficult, he continued, to frame such a constitution "as will be calculated for effectually promoting the general Good, making it the Interest of the Magistrates to prosecute the Prosperity of the People, and that of the People, to cultivate Reverence and Submission to their Superiors and Peace, concord & Harmony in the Community."[31] Allow even one error in the essential workings of those compacts and, like an error in the workings of a clock, the society will be engaged in endless disasters, according to Hardenberg. It seems that he was referring not only to the strife brewing to the north of New Jersey, but also to the conservative ideal of the deferential society—hardly a revolutionary position. Yet, Hardenberg was accounted an ardent patriot throughout the Revolution.

Jacob Green, Harvard graduate of 1744, explicitly asserted that the compact was the basis of government,[32] in a concise summary of Lockean theory. This compact had been broken, he concluded, and the colonies had thus become independent entities. Cooper included compact breaking as a valid reason for civil war,[33] and Carmichael implied a social compact when referring to "oaths and covenant" between the people and those "chosen by themselves to rule the whole."[34] Witherspoon, of course, reiterated the compact theory in his moral philosophy lectures.[35]

In contrast to the middle colony Reformed clergy who accepted, but gave small space to, the social compact and its corollaries, the compact received pronounced emphasis in the works of Locke, Sidney, and Milton.[36] Even if allowance is made for the difference in genres between sermon versus treatise or discourse, the bypassing of so prominent a group of interrelated concepts—consent, compact, representation—by the middle colony clergy is striking. It may be that these ideas were so commonly accepted that they were part of that vast, unspoken hinterland of belief held by all the colonists. One less elusive explanation might lie in the strength of these ministers' Calvinism, with its dogmatic stress on government having been ordained by God, and not just composed merely out of the consensus of men. They rarely argued that the king or his government was only a creation of his subjects.

Alternatively, perhaps, these preachers perceived that because the educational level or sophistication of their audiences was not high, the persuasive force of other issues would be greater. Thus, to effectively move their audience, they deemphasized the more abstract ideas in favor of the concerns being debated at every pub and street corner.

STANDING ARMIES: A NON-ISSUE

One issue *not* being argued about by the middle colony Reformed clergy was that of standing armies, unlike the importance attached to it by the fears of the eighteenth century commonwealthmen.[37] Only two of the middle colony preachers even mention it, and then only in passing.[38] This may be so because the middle colonies were geographically removed from those areas that were subject to the quartering of troops in peacetime. In any case, this suggests that the middle colony Reformed ministers were relatively unaffected by the English opposition writers, in contrast to New England clergymen, such as Andrew Eliot, who were vitally concerned about the threat posed by such armies.[39]

SUPREME POWER

The center of supreme power varied, according to the middle colony Reformed ministers that discuss it. Jacob Green simply stated that the magistrate has no authority but from the people. Enoch Green bluntly declared, "the King derives his power from the people."[40] Robert Cooper refuted the idea of Blackstone's that the supreme power, which must be lodged somewhere in any political body, was lodged in Parliament alone. Rather, the British constitution was a mixed government and that was where the supreme power lay.[41] For Parliament to formulate such an innovation as unlimited power over the people of the colonies was to "allege a metaphysical axiom against evident fact." Baptist David Jones removed the discussion entirely away from institutions. Jones interpreted the "higher powers" of Romans chapter 13 to be the "just, the good, the wholesome and constitutional laws of the land." These laws "ordained of God . . . must be like unto him," for "no law can make that just, which is in its own nature is unrighteousness." Jones added, "the people must be the judges whether the laws are good or not." And laws are good, he continued, only if they protect the property and lives of the people.[42]

Four leading Presbyterian ministers of Philadelphia advised their fellow believers in North Carolina of the proper stance to be taken towards the threatening civil war, and commented on the supreme power. They affirmed their allegiance to the king. On the other hand, they also wrote, "But it is said, that the Parliament of England has supreme power, and that no one ought to resist. This we allow, while they make Acts that are reasonable . . . they are limited by the laws of God and of reason . . . by the fundamental laws of the Constitution."[43] These four did not claim that the king's power was simply created by the people. Regardless of the exact center of power in these ministers' theories of government, they set forth most consistently the position that government is limited: no human institution can arrogate to itself the claim that it can rightfully bind its subjects in all matters whatsoever, as did the Declaratory Act.

Milton, in his 1650 *Tenure of Kings and Magistrates*, declared, "the power of kings and magistrates is nothing else but what is derived, transferred, and committed to them in trust from the people to the common good of them all, in whom the power yet remains fundamentally."[44] However, his motivation in that work was to justify removal or execution of a tyrant, not a just resistance to a tyrannous Parliament, as it was for the Reformed clergy of the middle colonies.

Locke may have been the source for the Reformed ministers' letter mentioned above, because he had written that the power of the supreme body of the nation, the legislature, was derived from the people, and, "the Supreame Power cannot take from any Man any part of his property without his own consent."[45] The Philadelphia ministers, in an almost parallel passage, wrote that "Parliament . . . may not enact that the King shall take the money of his English subjects without their consent."[46] On the other hand, the four ministers did not expressly state that Parliament derives its power directly from the people, nor that the ultimate power devolves back to the masses if they judge that the supreme power has acted tyrannically. Sidney, though, did assert that kings and governments are created rulers by the consent of the people, and that the supreme power remains in the whole people. They, and not the rulers, are masters of the law, and it is to the law that the people give allegiance;[47] this position is similar to the one that Jones advanced.

TYRANNY AND JUST WAR

Far more relevant to middle colony Reformed resistance ideology than arguments about the structure of government, were the twin concepts of just war and tyranny, which were also central arguments in earlier opposition political tradition.

The purpose of government, for the Reformed clergy, was to promote the welfare of the whole people, a duty most often defined as the protection of the lives, property, and religion of its subjects.[48] This purpose, of course, is one of the central themes hammered at by Locke, Sidney, and Milton.[49] For the middle colony ministers, tyranny was lawless, arbitrary oppression by a government that threatened their lives or property without cause,[50] essentially the same position taken by the seventeenth century political theorists.[51] However, the middle colony Reformed preachers advocated not the execution of the tyrant, but only a reversal of the situation, or a return to the status quo.[52] Locke, more conservative than Milton, allowed only that tyranny may be opposed or resisted so that the government might be dissolved, and the power to form a new government revert back to the people. Milton, on the other hand, maintained that tyrants should be deposed and punished, even executed, but only after all "means of redress" had been attempted. Sidney also condoned violence to remove tyrants; "seditions, tumults, and wars" were preferable to the desolation caused by tyranny.[53]

One problem associated with tyranny not solved by Locke, nor the other Republicans, was the tyranny of the majority. This majority-as-tyrant difficulty was "solved" in Locke's thought by merely asserting that the social compact included within it a tacit agreement to let the majority speak for all the decisions of the "body politick."[54] When this issue of minorities was addressed at all by the middle colony Reformed clergy—especially pressing in Pennsylvania because of the number of pacifists—two views were presented. Carmichael pleaded that those who were true Christian conscientious objectors must be tolerated, although they were to be pitied.[55] The majority agreed, however, that, under the conditions of war, those who chose not to join in resisting tyranny were "subversive of all peace and happiness," even of "all society and civil government."[56] Old Sider John Ewing, could not see, as the older Puritans also could not, that the pacifists were exercising precisely that right of dissent so precious to Puritans in England. Witherspoon argued that every society had to be determined by a plurality, and that everyone choosing to remain among them geographically after the start of hostilities tacitly gave his consent to that body.[57] The Reverend William Foster, after quoting Jeremiah 48:10, inverted Christ's words from Luke 9:50: "There can be, strictly speaking, no neutrality in the present case—he that is not with us must be against us."[58] At the extreme end of the spectrum, the four ministers of Philadelphia, including William Foster, even threatened Presbyterians turned Tory with excommunication and ostracism.[59]

The second major foundation of the middle colony Reformed resistance ideology was the just war theory, which will be covered more fully later, since for the middle colony Reformed it was founded on a theistic natural law base. In essence, these ministers justified resistance by portraying the acts of Parliament as an invasion of the rights of life and property and, especially the latter, as robbery. Similarly, civil war was justified by Locke as a response of the people against a tyrant, in the same way that armed resistance would be justified against a robber.[60] Milton also could not reckon civil war against a tyrant as a rebellion; rather, such a war merely did justice.[61]

RIGHTS OF ENGLISHMEN

While many arguments for resistance given by the middle colony Reformed could have been based largely on classical Republican writers' theories, the preachers' sermons were equally supported by Real Whig appeals to historical, legal-constitutional traditions. They appealed to their "natural and legal" rights as "men and Britons," i.e., "those derived from nature and our Ancestors."[62] The liberties which these ministers perceived as just as precious as their natural rights were those inherited from their Saxon forefathers: "British privileges and English liberty"; "The very genius of the British Constitution."

The ministers of Philadelphia and the Synod were specific as to what they regarded as those historical and constitutional precedents. They appealed to, besides natural law, the Magna Carta and the "fundamental laws of the Constitution." They contended, specifically, for the principles of the 1688 Glorious Revolution.[63] What they avoided was any claim to be ideological heirs of the Roundheads of the Good Old Cause, with one exception.

Presbyterian Enoch Green went beyond all the rest in that he specifically claimed that the colonists hoped to succeed simply because they were Whigs. "Little better than a century ago," said Green, the people "resisted and opposed a Tyrant, King Charles . . . [and] they took . . . their rights and vanquished the Tyrant." He asserted:

The Whigs have always gained the Day, the Tories have always been worsted, beat Charles I and took off his Head & James (the Pretender) & obliged him to flee to France, brought in K[ing] W, III and established the protestant Succession in the House of Hanover. And as long the House of Hanover were true to the Interest of the Whigs, Glory & Prosperity followed them. They were beloved by their subjects, successful in Warr and the Throne established. But now George has turned Tory. . . .[64]

But in general, the middle colony Reformed clergymen did not claim the Puritan revolution as the source of their historical rights. They were quite satisfied with the pre–Stamp Act status quo,[65] as even Enoch Green admitted elsewhere in the above sermon.

Although it is now impossible in most cases to pinpoint the exact sources, it can be said that the political arguments of the middle colony Reformed clergy for revolution correspond to those of the classical political theorists of the seventeenth century—Milton, Locke, and Sidney. On the other hand, the degree of influence of the eighteenth century commonwealthmen is far from clear, though certainly less than their known influence in New England. This latter conclusion can be inferred from the fact that there is no real evidence that their writings were known, much less required, reading in institutions where such would be expected.[66]

The middle colony Reformed argued for resistance on the basis of not only natural law and rights, but also their heritage as British subjects; constitutional government and fundamental law were their historical rights as Englishmen. On those bases, the middle colony Reformed presented a conservatively patriotic argument up to 1777, showing themselves willing to take up arms to resist, but not desiring to "dissolve the political bands" which held the colonies to Britain. They wished for a return to the status quo, though the economic and ideological pressures for independence might well have been too great for that in any case. Notably, both Old Side and New Side presented the same sort of conservative position. The historical-legal identification which they made with the English eventually became strained for they were no longer Englishmen, but Americans, a sense that was to develop as the decade passed.

Although Republican political thought may have influenced the resistance ideology of the middle colony Reformed clergy in the period of 1764 to 1782, these ministers were men zealously devoted to the Bible and Reformed theology. Theological considerations dominated their worldview. The next chapters will scrutinize the theological foundations of their resistance ideology.

5

Limits to Submission in the Middle Colonies

Standing alongside the New England patriot preachers in the western Christian traditions of just war and natural rights, the theologically conservative middle colony Reformed clergy also came to support armed resistance against the British Crown, although they endorsed it with a different style and emphasis of content. Their revolutionary sermons and tracts were characterized by a distinctive regionalism overlaid by a somewhat surprising application of the New England elect nation ideology to their pluralistic middle colonies. By this application, the middle colony Reformed ministers were able to use the genre of the Puritan jeremiad to urge colony-wide repentance and reformation for God's blessing and a quick end to the hostilities. By using that elect nation ideology they were also able to reinterpret the apocalyptic symbols of the book of Revelation: Britain was condemned as the Dragon and all the colonies, as well as New England, were defended as the Woman who fled into the (New World) Wilderness for refuge from civil and religious tyranny.

Moreover, if the passages in their works that seem to carry millenarian strains are scrutinized, a religious manifest destiny doctrine is apparent, not a civil millennialism based on Real Whig ideology. Fearing that various acts of the British authorities were corrupt attempts to truncate that manifest destiny—i.e., the westward expansion of the Kingdom of God under the auspices of a liberty-loving government—the middle colony Reformed clergy not only spurred on the colonial troops to greater valor, but also paid the price of resistance often with their estates and sometimes their lives.

NATURAL LAW OF SELF-DEFENSE

The rhetoric of the natural law of self-defense plays a prominent part in the middle colony Reformed sermons supporting revolution. Natural rights were those derived from natural law—a truism to the eighteenth century thinker regardless of his religious beliefs. To the Revolutionary era Reformed preachers, however, natural law was still held to be subsumed in the moral law of the Old Testament, as their theological tradition had affirmed all along,[1] and as their fellow patriot preachers in New England were even then proclaiming. For just one example, the Reverend William Foster quoted Scripture, and then said that the "simple voice of nature" would confirm it.[2]

In the Revolutionary period, middle colony Reformed clergy held that the self-preservation principle was inherent in human nature, placed there by God Himself. Robert Cooper said that that principle was "implanted in our natures, in common with other creatures," while Reverend John Carmichael wrote that it was "deeply engraved on the nature of every creature."[3] The supposition that God was the author and sustainer of natural law could, in the Reformed tradition, be traced to Calvin, who, when discoursing on civil government, wrote, "the law of God . . . the moral law is . . . natural law . . . which has been engraven by God on the minds of men."[4] However, self-defense was not a part of natural law in Calvin's system, but a development of earlier Roman Catholic and later Reformed traditions, as has been shown.

Natural law, frequently cited in middle colony sermons as a justification for revolution against tyranny,[5] was defined by Professor John Witherspoon as the dictates of general reason, i.e., "those obligations of duty from reason and conscience on one individual to another, antecedent to any particular law derived from the social compact."[6] But the quantum leap from that scholarly definition to the fiery resistance sermons, such as Robert Cooper's below, preaching revolution indicates that the middle colony Reformed clergy dealt with natural law in a manner tangential to historic Reformed theology.

Robert Cooper opens his three-point sermon by asserting that war was sometimes an unavoidable duty, citing the self-preservation principle deemed innate in humankind. After arguing that some wars and revolutions were illegitimate, he contends that Christians may engage in defensive revolution when rulers violate the original compact holding the nation together, i.e., "subvert the constitution . . . not for the good of the subjects, but to promote their own ambitious and tyrannical designs." Nonetheless, obedience is the first principle of politics for the believer, and use of the sword is the last resort. While denying that he was able to establish a line by which he could determine in all cases where "submission ought to end and resistance begin," Cooper does declare that that could be determined by "common necessity" rather than "casuistic divinity."

Historically, Reformed ministers writing on resistance reduced oppressive governmental actions to the level of personal felonies such as murder and robbery as discussed in earlier chapters. Cooper, following that Reformed tradition, asserts that, because of the innate natural law of self-preservation, the toleration of robbery and murder—this time by the British government agents—is absurd, for there "are certain rights derived from the God of nature." Furthermore, Cooper argues, also in line with his Reformed forefathers, to allow government officials to pillage and slaughter would be absurd, for the sole end of government is the good of its subjects. Civil rulers violating that purpose are guilty of cruelty, ingratitude, and perfidity, and "therefore, by the laws of nature, which can never be superseded, they deserve punishment, and it is sometimes necessary to remove them." And so, subjects carrying out that punishment and removal in a just and lawful way can expect God's favorable intervention on their behalf, for "if any interprize be a violation of the rights of our fellow-creatures," it is "consequently a breach of God's law."[7]

Cooper's and Foster's sermons are good illustrations of the endurance of the traditional Reformed identification of natural law with the moral law of the Bible,[8] and of self-defense being integrated with natural law. But, in addition, the middle colony Reformed clergy had transmuted the natural law of self-defense into more of a theory of natural rights. Overall, the moral law of the Bible was seen as the natural law of creation republished and clarified, and self-defense was seen as an integral part of this natural law, however rationalized and limited it had become through the thousand-year-old natural law/just war tradition.[9] Unfortunately, a critique of this transformation of natural law into natural rights would carry the discussion outside of historical analysis.

It would appear that the resistance ideology of the middle colony Reformed clergy fits Melvin Endy's perception of colonial revolutionary preaching, rather than Nathan Hatch's schema. Only four of the sermons examined equate the cause of colonial revolution with God's cause.[10] Furthermore, there is a distinction to be observed between asserting that "it is the cause of God we are engaged in" or that "the cause of America is the cause of Christ," and declaring that because the colonists' struggle was a just defense war, God would approve it and intervene on their behalf; the latter is more accurately the position of the middle colony Calvinists. It is also noteworthy that those four sermons, when raising the revolutionary struggle almost to the cosmic level, preceded those rhetorical equations with whole sections dealing with eschatological themes, as will be discussed later. After careful consideration, it must be concluded that the just war (not holy war) concept provided a primary reference point in the middle colony Reformed justification of revolution; the royalist doctrine of passive obedience and nonresistance had been explicitly rejected or, in their words, "exploded."[11]

LIMITS OF CHRISTIAN MEEKNESS

Though the natural law of self-defense continued to be an accepted part of Reformed theology in the colonies, some groups denied that Christians could participate in a war as combatants; the middle colony Reformed repudiated that pacifism with a traditional version of Christian self-defense. As a previous chapter has shown, the just war concept dominated the thinking of Christians when they reflected on responses to their countries' wars. From St. Ambrose to the present, as Roland Bainton has demonstrated, the great majority of Christians have either championed limited war or at least acquiesced to it.[12] This was particularly true of all the patriot preachers of the Revolutionary period, including the middle colony Reformed, and represents a major continuity of their resistance theory with the preceding eras. Long before the outbreak of hostilities, for example, Archibald Laidlie, a leading New York Dutch Reformed divine, had taught in a 1767 series of lessons on the Heidelberg Catechism that the sixth commandment "can't forbid a lawful war, as Socinians, Quakers, etc. imagine." Citing Exodus 22:2, he had justified self-defense for such an instance as when "a thief breaks through, etc."[13]

More specific than Laidlie's typical approval of the just war was its justification by Old Sider John Ewing in his Philadelphia sermons on Matthew 5:5, delivered in 1761 and 1767. Contrary to the popular view of Christian meekness, Ewing declared that to

> patiently suffer our religious rights and privileges to be invaded . . . without resistance . . . is so far from being a Branch of Christian Meekness that it is criminal in the sight of God. . . . As to our civil Rights and Privileges: to suffer others to invade them with impunity is to concur in the subversion of all society and civil government.

In response to Matthew 5:41, Ewing continued, "All then that is required of the meek by this precept is to bear lesser injuries in our reputation, property, or Liberty for the sake of peace as far as is consistent with our obligation to promote the welfare of the community."[14] Preaching on Matthew 5:10 in September 1766, Ewing singled out religious freedom as worthy of defense: to give up the rights of private judgment and conscience in religion, rather than to suffer, is to court divine displeasure.[15] Thus, at the community or national level there were to be limits to Christian meekness and deference.

When studying under Samuel Davies at the College of New Jersey, New

Sider Enoch Green wrote that "the meek will not take offense hastily and without just Reason, but be careful that they be not angry without Cause." Later, in the same theological notebook, he added that the meek also should be quick to be reconciled "when an offense is acknowledged, and reasonable Satisfaction offered."[16] Green was saying that Christian meekness, at the level of the individual, did have rational limits. Later, during the Revolution, he declared that those limits had been transgressed.

These theological-ethical statements defined neither the limits beyond which resistance should be undertaken by Christians nor the kinds of resistance that might be legitimate. Indeed, any statements by middle colony Calvinist clergy with explicit recommendations regarding resistance to political authority are rare before 1775. Such a rarity may simply be a result of the small size of the middle colony literary remains, as compared to that of New England; or, it may reflect a view of the ministry which usually denied any substantial place in sermons for partisan political messages.[17] Regardless, after the revocation of the Stamp Act, there was little reason to preach about resistance to authorities.

The scarcity of politically oriented sermons might also be seen as an echo of a general cultural and political conservatism. Both Old Side and New Side Presbyterians accepted the deferential class structure of mid-eighteenth century colonial America. For example, Ewing stated in 1767 that "in civil life, he [the meek] will study to behave with gentleness and respect to all according to their several ranks and stations in the world, rendering to all their due: tribute, custom, fear and honor to whom they are due."[18] Howard Miller, after having examined the educational system in force at the College of New Jersey during the colonial period, concluded that the New Side as well as the Old Side educated their students for a deferential society.[19] However, this deferential attitude in no way prevented expression of just war sentiments.

AMBIVALENCE TOWARDS RESISTANCE

In spite of the generally accepted views about submission and social class structure, the middle colony Reformed clergy before 1775 did occasionally speak to the political unrest of the colonies. Presbyterian James Sproat's July 1771 sermon, preached in Philadelphia (and repeated in August 1779, oddly without any detectable additions or changes in the manuscript), did not even mention armed resistance against the British. Rather, by recapitulating the historical persecution of the true church by Satan and his minions, Sproat managed to cast the whole sermon into an exhortation to be "deeply affected" by the church's "Distresses and Sorrows." What his listeners learned in the recapitulation was that when God sent "waisting Judgements"—famine, pestilence, and war—He was scourging "the wickedness of Nations, Empires, and Kingdoms."[20] Sproat hid oblique references to the political unrest in the country within a typical jeremiad form, merely instructing his listeners "to improve" upon what he had preached, while omitting any allusion to just war.

The Scottish ministers of the Associate Presbytery issued an *Act . . . for a Public Fast* in 1774 in which almost the entire text was taken up in cataloging, describing, and lamenting the sins of both England and the American colonies. Those sins were *the* cause of the political turmoil, which was euphemistically described as that "unhappy misunderstanding that presently takes place between Great Britain and her colonies."[21] These Calvinists did not even contemplate forceful resistance, for the cause of the political unrest was not, in their minds at that point, British tyranny, and for this reason, a just war was not possible. Theologically oriented, they sought ultimate causes, not secondary ones, just as did the English Puritans of the previous century.

The ambivalence toward armed resistance felt by the middle colony Reformed clergy in the transitional year of 1774 is well illustrated by a sermon by Presbyterian William Tennent, III, grandson of the founder of the Log College. In the preface, Tennent characterized the "Address" as "Equally adapted to the present State of the American colonies in general."[22] Although Tennent claimed "Political Subjects do not belong to the pulpit," yet, "to direct to right improvement of the times," preaching on that topic was a duty for every clergyman. The questions surrounding the "unnatural dispute" between Britain and the colonies reduced to either life as "Men and Britons" or "abject slavery."

Vacillating, Tennent then reiterated the inappropriateness of preachers of the gospel meddling with political issues: "It is beyond my Province and Inclination to enter into the Merits of this Controversy"; but, next, he warned that the "Cry of Oppression" is already heard in one corner of the land, and implied that it would soon be heard in all the colonies. After pointing out that "the first impulse" of those threatened by slavery and oppression is to strike back, and that God had promised to vindicate the oppressed, Tennent observed in an oblique threat that the use of violent means to remove oppression is "not inconsistent with the necessary principles of human nature, or contrary to the Word of God."[23]

Although Tennent probably would not have despised the just war, it was clearly not his purpose to defend it. He intended to drive home what to the Reformed clergy was the overriding problem of the land: sin, which had brought down God's chastening. He maintained, along with many others, that "It should be an invariable rule with Christians to regard the Hand of God in every Thing which happens, but especially in public Calamities."[24] With a similar mind-set, the Dutchess Presbytery of New York were praying in October 1774 that God would remove His wrath, "restore and continue to us our invaluable Privileges both civil and Religious, that most earnest Supplications be made for our King and all in authority, that under their wise and prudent administrations we may lead Quiet and peaceable lives in all godliness."[25] The reluctance of the Presbyterians to preach revolution was not just an individual position, but that of the denominational structures too.

As noted in an earlier chapter, the German Reformed clergy were explicitly loyal to the racially German King George II and his ministers. This kind of loyalty continued at least into the eighth decade of the eighteenth century. In 1770, the last part of the ordination pledges for one Reverend Bruin Comingoe asked, "Finally, do you acknowledge his Majesty the King, George the Third, and promise loyalty to him in all things pertaining to law and citizenship?"[26] He did affirm that, and was thence ordained to serve forty-nine years in Luneburg, Pennsylvania. However, an assessment of the German Reformed response to the political affairs of the early 1770s is very difficult for a number of reasons. These Germans were mostly poor and spread thinly throughout an agricultural region. A large number of those Germans that were located in the cities were indentured servants, some might say slaves.[27] In addition, they lacked German-language printing presses proportionate to their numbers in Pennsylvania, approximately 100,000.[28] There is no doubt, though, that eventually most of the German Reformed community, albeit not the pacifistic sectarians, joined the patriots' cause after the Revolution had actually begun.

In 1774, the Reformed clergy wobbled on the edge of a perceptual shift: but once hostilities had commenced, and a new government was set up by the Continental Congress, their preaching reflected that the shift had occurred. Though they still saw sin as the *ultimate* procuring cause of their country's "unnatural" dispute with Britain, the immediate causes of men and institutions assumed a new prominence in their messages—perhaps evidence of the impact of the Enlightenment worldview on the clergy. However, Reformed reluctance to condone revolution against the Crown was evident even in sermons delivered after Lexington and Concord.

The strength of the traditional Christian position is shown, for example, by Presbyterian Robert Cooper's assertion that the first principle of the Christian response to government is obedience, even under infidels or apostate believers,[29] the cornerstone of historical Reformed political ethics. Reverend John Carmichael in 1775, even while demonstrating that participating in a defensive war or revolution was legitimate for the Christian, told his Pennsylvania militia that they must still "observe . . . allegiance" to the king; furthermore, he said, "We do in America, all declare ourselves the subjects of King George, the third."[30] Fellow Presbyterian Joseph Montgomery, after justifying revolution, exhorted the officers of his unit to pray not only for themselves, but also for "mercy to the British nation, that God would bless our King."[31]

A group of Presbyterian ministers, which included Francis Alison and his revivalist rival George Duffield, in 1775 remonstrated that they did not seek independence.[32] The Dutchess Presbytery of New York, in May of 1775, was lamenting that God had caused "the Nation to be distracted with a Spirit of Discord and Contention" and "our Civil and Religious Priviledges to be invaded"; it called upon its people to repent and pray that wickedness might be repressed, vital piety promoted, discord subsided, unanimity restored, and "a lasting Union established," though it had to be, they added, "upon a Just and equitable Basis." The Huguenot church of New York also continued producing jeremiads up to the time of the invasion of their city.[33]

As late as 1776, Enoch Green, who had written theoretically of Christian meekness as a student, declared in a vehement camp sermon that the colonists did not desire independence, but, he added, his listeners should still make at home the basic ingredients for gunpowder.[34] Three months after independence had been declared, it was reported to William Smith that patriot Dutch domine Eilardus Westerlo was still offering up prayers for the King.[35] The middle colony Reformed clergy, in 1775, and perhaps beyond, were ambivalent about revolution, as were many political leaders of that period. Nevertheless, while a general political and social conservatism could account for a large portion of their reticence to preach revolution, there are indications that two other factors may have influenced their perspective.

FACTORS ENHANCING MIDDLE COLONY CONSERVATISM

James Sproat concluded his 1771 sermon by thanking God that "Indeed, at present we in this part of God's Church are exempted from the persecuting of its Enemies. We have leave to worship God according to our consciences. Each one to sit under our Vine and under our Fig Tree and none to make us afraid."[36] This statement indicates that the irritants, threats, and actual economic hardships imposed upon New England had not yet been felt by the middle colony Reformed communities. Similarly, William Tennent's 1774 comment that the "Cry of Oppression is already heard in one Corner of the Land,"[37] implies that the middle colony "corner" was still relatively unaffected by the tightening grip of the British administration. In 1775, John Carmichael could still say to the Pennsylvanian militia,

> You are, in this town, now at ease, in the lap of peace and plenty, far from any sense of either blood or slaughter—in the heart of a rich province situated in the center of the whole American continent—you hear of distress, but you do not yet feel it . . . as some . . . now do in Boston.[38]

In the colonial period, the distance between Boston and Philadelphia made a world of difference economically, socially, and politically. Not only the ethnically British but, according to Arthur Graeff, also the Pennsylvania Germans were unaffected by the economics of the Intolerable Acts of 1766–74. An episcopalian establishment never was a serious threat in their pluralistic colony.[39] Thus, one factor that allowed the middle colony Reformed clergy the luxury of a longer period of political conservatism may have been simply a relative geographic and economic isolation from the New England complex and its perturbations following military occupation by the British.

The other factor reflected in the middle colony Reformed clergy's literature was a "malignant advisors" theory, analogous to that propounded by the English Puritan clergy of the 1640s decade.[40] Reverend Carmichael told colonial troops in 1775: "Your drawing the sword now must not be against the person of his Majesty, but the maladministration of his government by designing, mischief-making ministers." It was "the present Ministry" that was "determined to cram disloyalty and disobedience down our throats . . . call us rebels—then confiscate our country and sell it. . . ."[41] Decrying the absolute inclusiveness of the Declaratory Act—which is mentioned far more often in the middle colony Reformed sermons than any other of the Intolerable Acts[42]—Robert Cooper asserted that the Act would make the colonists "not merely subjects of the Imperial Crown of Great Britain, but slaves of the Parliament of Great Britain." The king was not singled out as a tyrant, rather "the late acts of the British Parliament . . . have at length brought on a civil war."[43] In the same year as Foster's sermon, Joseph Montgomery, alluding to the Exodus, declared,

> there has arose up a new King who seems not to know us as his children and subjects. His servants, the Ministers of state led by mistaken principles, or actuated by interested motives, seem jealous of the rising glory and are frightened at . . . the future greatness of America . . . unconstitutional statutes are formed by the parliament of Great Britain . . . our charters are only like walls of paper, insufficient to screen us from Ministerial vengeance.[44]

Even as late as February of 1776, at least to Reverend William Foster, the "bloody Ministry and packed Parliament" were the ones who had attempted to enslave the colonists in order to support "swarms of court sycophants and hungry leeches."[45] The king had been, according to the 1775 pastoral letter of the Presbyterian Synod, misled by his court.[46] Apparently many of the Reformed ministers in this early Revolutionary period felt compelled to shift the charge of tyranny away from the king himself to the Parliament, just as the British Puritans had done in the seventeenth century.

Regardless of the inherent conservatism of the middle colony Reformed clergy, the relative economic and geographic isolation from New England and its problems, and the theory that the Revolution was a misunderstanding or a court-led deception of George III, the reluctance of the middle colony Reformed to preach armed resistance was overcome decidedly in the first place because of the perception that the struggle fulfilled just war criteria.

TRIUMPH OF REVOLUTIONARY SENTIMENT

While some middle colony Reformed clergy were content to assert merely that the Revolution was just,[47] others cited more specific criteria. The one criterion most often asserted was "last resort." The Reformed clergy felt that the colonists had made every attempt at reconciliation with Great Britain, short of appeasement. Their resort to the sword was an appeal to God to decide the justice of their cause.[48] Furthermore, not only was the colonists' cause just, but also the means employed by the British in prosecuting the war were unjust. The latter had hired mercenaries to plunder civilians in the countryside, and had starved their prisoners.[49] Of even more propaganda value was the kind of graphic letter to the newspapers Reverend Alexander MacWhorter wrote, detailing murder, rape, and robbery by British men and officers in 1777.[50]

Most specific, in reference to the unjust means used by the British, was a 1778 letter written by Dutch Reformed domines John Leydt and Reynier Van Nest on behalf of a large portion of the colonial Dutch church to the classis of Amsterdam. Leydt and Van Nest justified not only the lack of communication between the two bodies, but also Dutch patriots' support of the Continental Congress. The domines had chosen armed resistance because it was a just cause. They were confirmed in that choice when they heard of the "inhuman treatment of so many thousands of our prisoners," the "wanton burning" of their towns and homes, the robbing of civilians, the murdering of noncombatants, and "above all, the mallacious and God-provoking destruction of our churches."[51] All of these acts were violations of the 'rules' formulated by just war theorists.

Earlier than the Dutch communique above, and of great interest because of its singularity, was the forty-page pamphlet of August 1775 from the Lutheran and Reformed church officials in Philadelphia, *Schreiben des Evangelisch-Lutherisch und Reformirten Kirchen-Raths . . . an die Teutschen Einwohner* of New York and North Carolina. These Lutheran and Reformed clergymen and elders urged support of the colonial Congress for several reasons and reprinted in German the Congressional "Declaration on Taking Up Arms," the "Address to the Inhabitants of Great Britain," and the "Petition to the King," authored by John Dickinson. These ministers, presided over by one Louis White, believed that the taking up of arms was a legitimate response to the "encroachment" on their rights and freedoms.[52] The English, they declared, had scorned the colonials as "poltroons" and "boors" from whom they thought they could bloodlessly steal through taxation. They had invaded New England, killed at Lexington, and then burnt Charleston. Similar to the French in earlier decades, the British had fomented the Indians against the colonists, inciting those whose barbarities were still "in the fresh memory of all of our adult men."[53]

Throughout the pamphlet, there was a notable disinclination to indict the king directly. Rather, the agents or sources of oppression were Parliament, but even more the king's servants or "ministers of state." Indeed, the king, as presented in this pamphlet, seems guilty, at most, of the irresponsibility of passing on to Parliament for disposition the petitions of Congress. Even though the best British orators had declaimed in favor of the colonial cause, yet the "plan of the royal ministers" was passed by Parliament. The Lutheran and Reformed authors of this pamphlet singled out General Thomas Gage as a special target for their clerical rage.[54]

What is absent, as might be expected for a pamphlet directed to non-English-speaking ethnic Germans, is any identification with Puritan forefathers such as that contained in the attached Congressional addresses and other Reformed clergy's sermons. Rather, the emphasis was upon identification of the Congress as the legitimate leaders of the colonies, and upon identification with the colonists at large in what they were suffering at the hands of the British. The Congressional delegates were the *duly* authorized representatives of the *united* twelve colonies.

The British were attempting "to deprive us of freedoms enjoyed since the beginning of our building up of these lands, and to make us slaves of Parliament or to kill us with fire and sword . . . as rebels and traitors."[55] Perhaps the king, as the symbol of stability and authority, was too dear emotionally to attack directly. Perhaps formal argumentation about such things as natural law, the social compact, or virtual representation would not have aroused many German farmers. Regardless, this pamphlet did enumerate reasons which fit easily the just war theory, and it was well targeted to the German Reformed agricultural community.

What made the colonists' cause just in the eyes of the Reformed clergy was the fact that it was a defensive revolution. They were *defending*, just as the seventeenth century English Puritans claimed they were defending, their lives, civil and religious liberties, and, especially, properties.[56] Self-defense was a natural right, based on natural law, and was legitimate for appropriation by Christians regardless of whether they were Dutch, German, English, or Scots in origin, because it was seen to be condoned by the Scriptures, especially the Old Testament. The natural law of self-defense formed the greatest continuity of the middle colony Reformed resistance ideology with historical Reformed resistance theory. What had developed, however, was a slightly altered form of that natural law: now a natural *right* of self-defense was held up as justification for revolution.

6

To Protect God's Covenant People

PROVIDENTIAL MEANS

In addition to the just war, the middle colony Reformed clergy conscripted the more purely theological concepts of divine providence and human means to bolster their patriotic resistance sermons. They asserted that God both chastised and vindicated His people through "ordinary" or secondary means. Even though by the corrupt passions of malevolent men God was working out His divine purposes,[1] the means chosen to wage a just war must be "proper" or "appointed" means.[2] Secondary means, such as human warfare, *had* to be used, for the age of miracles had ceased.[3] This was not to say that God did not intervene directly into human affairs by earthquakes, storms, and pestilence, but that most often, men were given only the Scriptures for guidance, and their own Spirit-led actions for producing results. God acted directly on their minds to produce certain attitudes and imaginations which would lead to particular actions, leading, in turn, to victory or defeat. In other words, God directed His people to use means, and made those means effectual.[4]

On the one hand, the patriot preachers legitimized the means of armed warfare and demonstrated the justice of their revolution, thus undermining the positions of both the pacifists and the Tories. In doing so, they appear to have targeted the undecided moderates with rhetoric seemingly calculated to polarize their audience. For most of the Reformed clergy, there could be no neutrality under conditions of war.[5] Some argued that not only was the general "alternative . . . to wear the chain or the sword," but in particular, that their hearers were to be either for the colonists—the persecuted people of God—or for the British.[6]

On the other hand, the middle colony Reformed warned of the common danger of undue exaltation of the secondary instruments of God's providence. Robert Cooper, for example, summarized the enduring Scylla and Charybdis of the providential worldview in the following way: to trust in means alone and neglect seeking God is pride and atheism; to pretend to trust God, and at the same time to neglect the use of proper means, is foolish presumption and wild enthusiasm.[7] Clearly, for the middle colony Reformed, to refrain from use of proper means was sinful, but to displace God, even with legitimate means, was also heinous. God had to be given the glory for any military victories, even when some of his human agents were also lauded.[8]

In their providential worldview, God judged the actions of not only the individual, but also nations. At times He extended mercy, but at other times wrath. These preachers distinguished the Lord's judgments of individuals from those of nations by averring that individuals might receive full recompense for their sins in the life hereafter, whereas nations must drink the full cup of wrath in this world, for they will not exist in the world to come.[9] As George Duffield preached in relation to Nehemiah 9:26–27: "When such is the character of a people," that "judgment may be expected—there is in the economy of God's providence a moral necessity of it." To allow sin to go on indefinitely would impugn God's divine moral government and appear to encourage sin.[10]

The Dutch Reformed pastor John Henry Livingston seems even more certain than Duffield, for the former wrote that though the ways of providence were obscure for the individual, there was "one general uniform mode" of God's judgment of a nation. For Livingston, "there are certain national virtues which brings national blessings, and national sins which produce national evils."[11] Notably, the sins for which nations earned God's wrath were also those for which individuals were to be condemned, which constitutes a possible weakness in their argument. They were nonetheless certain that God hated America's sins, and that the war was His means of demonstrating that hatred.

In general, the doctrinal basis is less than clear for the middle colony Calvinist clergy's declaration that God was judging America for her sins. One approach was a kind of general natural law for nations, such as propounded by John Henry Livingston above.[12] All nations were judged alike in *this* world for the same sins. At another level, however, these preachers held to a special kind of people-of-God culpability. Duffield's sermon on Nehemiah 9:26–27 makes clear that, though he held to the inevitability of judgment for nations because of the moral underpinnings of God's creation, he was preaching to God's people and applying that general theory to America in a unique way. Unfortunately, at times, the distinction between the nations and the people of God was blurred when pronouncing or explaining the judgment seen in the war.[13]

The middle colony Reformed ministers' doctrine of God's nonmiraculous providence, combined with their view of the instinct of self-preservation, necessarily led to a strong emphasis on human means. Though the elevation of human means and abilities might possibly be seen as simply expedient exploitation of theology for ideological purposes, or less negatively, the result of Enlightenment perceptions of human nature, both their doctrines of providence and of the natural law of self-defense formed clear continuities with the previous centuries of Reformed thought. The deciding factor which tipped their preaching towards support of revolution was an appropriation for the middle colonies of the New England elect nation ideology.

APPROPRIATION OF THE ELECT NATION IDEOLOGY

Far more striking than the continuities considered previously, is the extent to which the middle colony Reformed simply appropriated the religious heritage of the New England Puritans and, then, applied the latter's convenanted Christian nation ideology to the pluralistic middle colonies. Again and again, statements appear such as, the "Lord has a controversy" with "His people,"[14] or God led His people—the colonists—to this howling "wilderness" and preserved them there far from tyranny,[15] or that America prophetically fulfilled the place of the Woman of Revelation fled from the Dragon.[16] Not once in all these Reformed sermons and tracts was it questioned whether this appropriation was valid. While the repetition of motifs, symbols, and allusions are suggestive of what might have influenced the middle colony Reformed when preaching revolution, more indicative of their motivations are the concrete identifications they made with the New England Puritans.

Toward the end of his 1774 presidential commencement address at Queen's College, Dutch domine Jacob R. Hardenberg (1736–90) asked his audience to join him in hoping

> that a benign Lord, who by his kind hand of Providence, transplanted *our valient Ancestors* from the eastern to this western once inhospitable Continent may go on to preserve and establish our dear bought Liberties, handed down to us by *our glorious Ancestors*. O' may America never want Sons . . . to defend her civil and religious liberties, and promote the public weal of the present and rising Generation. That the degenerate Sons of better Ancestors may . . . bask themselves in the sunshine of Privilidges their Fathers have acquired at the expence of their Blood and Treasure.[17]

At this time, the middle colonies were nowhere near to declaring revolution as were the New England colonies. Yet, Hardenberg, ethnic Dutch though he was, here straightforwardly identifies himself and his listeners with the New

England Puritans. Now, it is not known what the composition of his audience was (only one young man graduated in the class of 1774), but unless his speech was purely rhetorical, it indicates that not only the Dutch Reformed domines of a non-Dutch background—Laidlie, Livingston, and Linn—had appropriated the Puritans for their religious heritage, but at least some of the ethnic Dutch clergy also.

Another domine, John Henry Livingston, when preaching to his Dutch Reformed congregation on an official day of thanksgiving in 1777, recounted the many gracious interpositions God had performed in order to save the colonists from defeat. During his recollection, he developed parallels between Britain and Egypt, and America and Israel; the situation for the colonists in his city, then, was "as in the days of Israel." During the first part of the parallel, Livingston declares that "the same Revolution" occurred "in Britain as with Pharoah." But then, before highlighting more current events of the siege, he plainly states, "First [they] drive us out from them—by their own cruel laws."[18] This reference amounts to an identification of his Dutch Reformed community with the New England Puritans.

Since this message was an unpublished sermon preached originally to his New York Dutch congregation, there was no editing of it for publication, and thus, it is all the more telling about how he, and probably his parishioners, felt about their place in the war. Livingston had legitimized Dutch colonists rebelling against the British authorities by appropriating the English Puritans' historical immigration experience, which, in turn, had been legitimized by associating it with the history of ancient Israel. However, lest too much be made of two isolated manuscript addresses by Dutch Reformed clergymen, other sources of this kind of resistance theology should be examined.

Reverend William Foster, in 1776, tied together a particular perspective on the fulfillment of prophecy, and a Puritan Exodus theology, as premises for the radical question, "Who would not run the risk of spilling some blood for the enlargement of Christ's mystical body the Church?" First, Foster asserted that Britain was God's elect nation, and, then, applied to it passages of Scripture that, in their original sense, applied only to Israel. Britain was, in turn, then rejected for its sins, and judged accordingly. Next Foster applied to the American colonies Scriptures that originally had meaning only for Israel (Psalms 80:9–10).[19] God had made America His vineyard, His elect, and "surely" did not intend for the Gospel to be bottled up along the eastern seaboard. "America," asserted Foster, "*corresponds* to the account we have of the wilderness to which the Church was driven to seek protection from the fury of the Dragon, Revelation 12:13–14." This passage, he wrote, had an *"eminent* fulfillment" when "our ancestors fled."[20] Foster took the New England congregational Puritans as his forebears and those of his middle colony, Presbyterian congregation. The status of God's new elect nation, New England, expanded to the middle colony community, which by a leap, became heirs to the New England fulfillment of the "prophecy" of Revelation.

Revivalist George Duffield, when preaching in 1776 to his Philadelphia congregation, declared that it was "Our forefathers who first inhabited yonder eastern shores" that "fled from . . . tyranny."[21] Indeed, it was the "spirit [of liberty] that inspired our forefathers' breasts, when first they left their native shores, and embarked for this then howling desert."[22] Like Foster and Livingston, and in spite of the fact that Presbyterianism had had a substantial middle colony presence only in the eighteenth century, Duffield not only ardently defended the right of revolution, but also looked to the New England Puritan experience for the historical identity of his audience. In similar language, Joseph Montgomery asked his countrymen to allow him

> to observe then, that in the reign of Charles the First, and . . . of the succeeding Princes of the . . . Stuarts, tyrannical power was exercised in Great-Britain, and the most unjust encroachments made upon the sacred rights of the nation. Many of our forefathers groaned under bondage not inferior to that of Egypt . . . Liberty had . . . set up her standard in the wilds of America. [Our forefathers] hoped . . . that neither civil nor ecclesiastic tyranny would pursue them to this then howling wilderness.[23]

Identification with the New England Puritans allowed the middle colony patriots to preach that the British "encroachments" in their day were a revival of the tyranny perpetrated upon the Puritans in the previous century. Because of the perception that the fertile planting of the New England Puritans was God's benevolent doing, it was a small step in logic to conclude that for the British to curb development of the colonies was to attack God's workings in the middle colonies also. Thus, the right to resistance was infused with a righteous wrath.

REVOLUTION FOR POSTERITY'S SAKE

In order to fuel revolutionary fires, the middle colony Reformed clergy also painted in glowing colors the future of their country. Frequently, they exhorted their listeners to resist the British for the sake of their posterity and the benefits that would accrue to it.[24] For example, Joseph Montgomery, preaching in Pennsylvania at the start of the revolution, suggested that "the happiness of thousands, yet unborn may depend upon your conduct";[25] later, in 1778 in New Jersey, Jacob Green declared, "we are engaged in a glorious cause: We are nobly contending for the good of millions yet unborn."[26]

Toward the end of hostilities, Robert Smith said that the colonists were obliged to praise God for their approaching victory; "Those obligations arise from the nature and importance of the cause contrasted with the fatal consequences to us and our posterity had we lost."[27] The middle colony Reformed ministers had in their own minds, and kept before their parishioners, a vivid picture of the historic importance of their struggle, a struggle that would determine the living conditions of their children's children. Revolution was worth defending for the sake of future potential blessings.

REVOLUTION TO PROTECT THE WORLD'S ASYLUM

The Reformed clergy dovetailed their concern for the future benefits of the Revolution accruing to their own children with their perception of the unique place or role of America as an "asylum" for all mankind. However, this perception did not begin solely as part of a revolutionary resistance ideology. As early as 1763, Francis Alison was preaching in Philadelphia that the "grand designs" of Christ had "here opened an asylum for persecuted protestants for all denominations."[28] Dutch Reformed minister Archibald Laidlie, just shortly before the Declaration of Independence, hoped that after the colonists had repented, God would vindicate their cause and "shew to Europe, to the world that he has chosen America as the happy place where not only civil Liberty, but true Religion shall flourish in spite of all our enemies."[29]

In the same year as Laidlie, George Duffield declared, "This western world appears to have been . . . designed by an ordinance of heaven as an ASYLUM for LIBERTY, civil and religious."[30] In the middle years of the war, chaplain Israel Evans imagined a tearful, personified America wondering, "And have I not, when she [liberty] was excluded from every other region of the earth opened the arms of my protection, and received the persecuted stranger to my friendly and virtuous shores?"[31]

Looking into the future from 1781, Robert Smith foresaw that America would "yet be a refuge to many European saints from the dreadful storm, when God shall cast down thrones, and deluge Europe with blood, to prepare the way for the promised glory of the latter days."[32] God had chosen, guided, and prepared the land of America for providential blessings of religious and civil liberties throughout the colonial period, and because it was protecting those blessings for both their posterity and future immigrants, the Revolution could only be righteous.

The middle colony Reformed clergy's adoption of the biblical Exodus motif and Puritan New England themes, along with the concern for the freedoms of their posterity, are clues for further scrutiny of those passages with millennialistic themes. Not only had God chosen America as an "asylum" for the oppressed of the earth fleeing tyranny, but He had chosen it as the unique place from which the Kingdom of God would spread over all the continent, and then the whole world. It is here that one can see the real connection between the Great Awakening and the American Revolution. Foundational to the middle colony Reformed preaching of armed revolution was the hope of the Kingdom of God on earth: they preached their just revolution in order to protect the ongoing spread of that kingdom. These clergymen had developed more of a Christian "Manifest Destiny" ideology for which men should willingly sacrifice, rather than a "civil millennialism" in which the "ultimate goal of apocalyptic hope—the conversion of all nations to Christianity—had become diluted with, and often subordinate to, the commitment to America as a new seat of liberty," as Hatch has claimed for the preaching of the New England clergy.[33]

REFORMED RELIGIOUS MANIFEST DESTINY

The development of this Christian Manifest Destiny ideology was expanded in the period of 1763 to 1781. In his 1763 sermon of thanksgiving for the peace treaty, Francis Alison declared that the "pride and ambition" of France "has been so observed by Providence that we see popery has gotten the mortal blow in north America, and there is opened a fair and unexpected prospect that the Protestant religion will extend to the north pole and to the Russian seas." Later in the same work, he saw for Britain "a glorious prospect of her colonies enlarging the Kingdom of Christ"; he concluded his lengthy piece with the exhortation:

> Let us thank God for the fair and extensive prospects which we now have that the Kingdom of Christ shall flourish in north America and his name shall be great among the heathen nations, and O let us improve this unspeakable blessing by loving God, by loving one another, by promoting the conversion and welfare of the Indian nations, by preserving and prizing our privileges civil and religious, and by showing kindness to our distressed friends and country-men who are driven from their dwellings and deprived of this blessing of peace.[34]

The middle colony Reformed clergy were contemplating the conversion of the whole continent to Christianity long before any tensions with the mother country.

Not long after Lexington and Concord, the Reverend John Carmichael concluded his sermon with the benediction, "may God grant that out of these present tumults, disturbances and commotions, a great and mighty empire may rise up in the western world, for King JESUS, as well as a Protestant King built on the solid principles of liberty and true religion."[35] Note which king is allocated first place.

Once patriots had initiated armed combat for independence, the middle colony Reformed clergy defended revolution for the purposes shown above, while they also rejoiced at the possibility of an ever-widening Kingdom of God in America. Reverend William Foster gave the colonists reasons as to how they were to "judge of God's being on our side, to fight our battles." He observed, "Now surely God did not make such a large share of our globe for nought, or only to be the haunts of . . . naked untutored Indians. . . . we may believe that God designs the settlement of its remotest boundaries for the enlargement of his son's kingdom."[36]

George Duffield, even prior to the Declaration of Independence, stated that Christ's kingdom in America had made great strides already, and, in face of the British threat, queried, "shall his foes tear the laurels from the brow of the great Redeemer? and deliver his victory and glorious prospects into slavery and thraldom! Forbid it Jesus, from thy throne!" Duffield was certain "the Church shall flourish here and hold on her way triumphant, in spite of Kings, Lords, Commons, and Devils, until yonder vast unexplored western regions shall all resound the praises of God." Moreover, he justified the approaching revolution because to him the Kingdom of God was the most important movement on earth, and "as civil and religious liberty live or languish together, so shall the civil liberty of America *hold pace with* the triumphs of the Gospel through out this extensive land."[37] Here, civil liberty, though tied to religious liberty, is subordinate to it.

As the war continued, middle colony Reformed clergy continued to preach its justice and to justify it in connection with the increase of Christ's kingdom. In 1778, the Scottish Calvinists of the Associate Presbytery issued a pamphlet in which they prayed that God would fill the colonial leaders with the Holy Spirit and wisdom so that they could successfully prosecute the "present just and necessary war, 'til it shall please God to grant us a safe and honourable peace," with "the full and lasting enjoyments of all our rights and liberties, both sacred and civil."[38] But, they preceded this prayer by saying that "in the mean time we have good reason to hope that he will give a revival to his work in this large continent . . . that he will build Zion in this land."[39] That prayer for an end to hostilities was followed by another prayer "that he may hasten the more eminent glory of the latter days," specifically "the destruction of the Anti-Christian state, the downfall of Mahometan tyranny and delusion, the enlargement of the Mediator's kingdom among the Jews and Gentiles, and the revival of his work in the Church."[40]

Jacob Green, whose mid-war patriotic jeremiad included just war theory, concern for their posterity, and Puritan motifs, declaimed, "What a happy land this will be, if," after vindication of the Revolution, America " 'tis a land of true religion! It will be a land of liberty, of peace, and plenty." Like a city set on hill, "many from other nations will flock to us as the most happy people on the face of the earth."[41] Clearly, for Green the future religious role of America was not subordinate to its political arrangements. Rather, in his view of organic society, civil liberties were coordinate with the religious vitality of its people.

This perspective of a coordinate role of the civil and the religious achievements of a people was also reflected in a sermon by Israel Evans, who defended the Revolution from within the context of a religious Manifest Destiny for America. He concluded his exhortation to the troops by observing that the "Gospel, or Sun of Righteousness has only glanced on the shores of this western world, and it is predicted of it, that it shall be universally propagated . . . [and] like the Sun, travel to the western extremities of this continent." Thus, "how happy" the colonial troops should be "to have been the instruments . . . of God, for accomplishing so great a revolution, and extending the Kingdom of His Son so far. Liberty and religion shall have their wide dominion from the Atlantic through the great continent to the western ocean."[42]

Old Sider Matthew Wilson in the same year undertook a detailed patriotic exposition of prophecy in the book of Revelation and perceived in it the events of the American Revolution. But in his summation, when praying that the Lord God would pour out the seventh vial of judgment, what Wilson foresaw as results of that prophecy for America was not a *novo ordo seculorum*, but "vengency to be executed on Satan . . . in order to accomplish a glorious reformation, which we hope will first begin in America, where the beast of religious establishments is forever rejected. That Jews and Gentiles may become real and vital Christians, and a kind of heavenly Paradise, the seventh Chiliad," might come about, "which period we next expect, and fully believe on the faith of sacred prophecy."[43] While during his exposition Wilson presents civil and religious liberties as an inseparable pair,[44] nowhere does he straightforwardly identify them (either sacralizing the political or secularizing the religious), nor does he subordinate the religious to the civil.

Near the end of hostilities, Robert Smith set down in Pennsylvania what gave him hope for success in the war and for "future glorious days to America." Not only was the flight of the Puritan "forefathers" to New England a fulfillment of Revelation 12, but, in addition, the "operations of providence united with the predictions of the gospel shining as lightening from the east to the west" presaged victory in the struggle for independency.[45] However, he concluded, "The strongest of all my reasons was the everlasting promise of . . . the Father to the Son, Psalm 2:8. . . . O' America . . . glory shall have her habitation in you! Happy shall it be to have a place among you."[46] While Smith would probably have been an adherent to many of the tenets of real

Whiggery, his vision of a millennialistic Kingdom of God overshadowed his political beliefs.

When middle colony Reformed ministers like Wilson and Evans joined together both civil and religious concerns in talking of liberties, it might appear that some variety of civil millennialism was operating in their minds. Indeed, there were millennial themes in their sermons and tracts. However, the accepted truth among most political and religious thinkers in the eighteenth century was that civil and religious freedoms stood or fell together. Society was perceived then as being more organic than it is now. Professor John Witherspoon, in 1776, could have been speaking for every one of the middle colony Reformed clergy when he said at the College of New Jersey:

> The knowledge of God and his truths have from the beginning of the world been chiefly, if not entirely confined to those parts of the earth where some degree of liberty and political justice were to be seen, ... there is not a single instance in history in which civil liberty was lost, and religious liberty preserved entire. If therefore we yield up our temporal property, we at the same time deliver the conscience into bondage.[47]

Because the Church, in these men's ecclesiology, was very much *in* the world even if not of it, and because most of them held to a kind of postmillennialism, the protection of civil liberties was paramount to safeguard religious freedom. The middle colony Reformed were vitally interested in the conversion of the continent, and they defended the Revolution because of their perception of the threat to extension of the Kingdom of God. However, with rare exceptions, the struggle with the British was not defined as a struggle between the people of God and Satan or the Antichrist.[48]

The British had, though, already acquiesced to Catholic hegemony in Quebec, and this brought back to Reformed communities bitter memories of war against the instruments of Antichrist.[49] The ill-treated German Reformed pastor, John Zubly, even publicly communicated to the Earl of Dartmouth the opinion that many Americans saw the Intolerable Acts of the British Ministry as measures to bring in the Catholic pretender.[50] The specter of religious establishment was at least present in the minds of middle colony Reformed clergy before, during, and after the Revolution,[51] and Carl Bridenbaugh has made a considerable case for the fear of Anglican establishment (at least in New England) as being one of the motivations for revolution. But the sermons examined here show that the fear of Anglican establishment was not a major, publicly articulated fear to the middle colony Reformed clergy.

The middle colony Reformed ministry's justification of armed resistance to the British authorities stood squarely in the Calvinist tradition of resistance thought. No government or ruler could claim to bind them "in all cases whatsoever" as the Crown-in-Parliament had decreed for itself; God alone was absolutely sovereign. Revivalists and Old Siders, Presbyterians, Baptists, and German and Dutch Reformed all came together to defend revolution on the basis of Scripture, especially the Old Testament, and on the theory of the just war, which was seen as based on the law of God, and, thus, a legitimate guide to the ethics of armed revolution.[52]

What was new in their particular case, as opposed to historical Reformed resistance thought, was their peculiar combination of eschatology and ecclesiology. The status of the New England Puritans as the chosen people of God was appropriated by the middle colony Reformed clergy and applied to the pluralistic middle colonies and the colonies of America as a whole. By assuming divine election for a particular mission—the extension of His Kingdom in America—the middle colony Reformed were able to develop a religious Manifest Destiny for America, i.e., the march westward of Christianity across the continent.

With the possibility of having that destiny thwarted by the British through civil or religious tyranny, the middle colony Reformed justified revolution from eschatological expectations as well as the more classical Reformed concepts. The middle colony Reformed had added to the classical Reformed defense of the right to revolution a further motivation: the prospect (strengthened by postmillennialism) of a new Zion in America, a completion, in their eyes, of the vision their spiritual forefathers had sought on New England's rocky coast generations before, and a fulfillment of the hopes motivating revivalists like Jonathan Edwards in the Great Awakening.

Not only did the extension of the concept of "God's covenant protestant people" to the whole middle colony community justify armed resistance when added to all the other facets of Reformed political ideology, but it also heightened a rising consciousness as Americans that had started in the Great Awakening. This extension, whether theologically legitimate or not, helped to develop the early nationalism of the nascent Republic. In that way, it galvanized all the people for the trials ahead.

7

Conclusions

The revolutionary preaching of the Reformed clergy of the middle colonies was based more significantly on the religious or theological beliefs of that ministerial group than has been appreciated, a conclusion already reached by some others in regards to New England revolutionary preaching. The middle colony Calvinists had little need to look for sources outside their own theological tradition, for it had already developed the major components of a rigorous resistance ideology. To motivate resistance to the British Crown, the Reformed clergy harnessed two of the oldest currents of western intellectual history: the natural law of self-defense and the just war, both already accepted parts of Reformed political ideology.

These clergymen accepted as fact the idea that a natural law existed which was authored and instilled into the human soul by God Himself; these ministers deemed self-preservation a part of that law, following Christian theologians from at least Aquinas on. Although they also accepted the Reformed tradition's doctrine of depravity and its judgment that natural law was theologically useless except to make man inexcusably guilty before God, they did believe that, in the public arena, natural law was useful for general guidance of the body politic through the agency of magistrates and rulers. However, for the most part the Reformed clergy assumed that the magistrates would be confessing Christians; thus, the latter would be guided by the Scriptures—the natural law clarified—rather than the dim residual of natural law available to depraved pagans.

The natural law of self-defense could be invoked and revolution justified when the agents of government ceased to carry out either of its divinely mandated purposes: the welfare of the subjects of the land, or the protection of the church and its mission to spread the Kingdom of God. Because the middle colony Reformed firmly maintained the historical Reformed perception that the moral law of the Bible was clarified natural law, the authority with which self-defense and its socio-political extrapolate, just war, could be invoked matched that of the Gospel. The great weight given to the natural law of self-defense in their justifications of war and revolution may explain why there is no apparent difference between revivalists and anti-revivalists in war ideology, an aspect missed by Alan Heimert.

The perturbation of middle colony Reformed revolutionaries from the doctrine of submission to political authorities was provoked by historical circumstances, that in some ways paralleled the situation surrounding the English civil wars. While by the time of the Revolution, the threat to American Reformed Christianity from Roman Catholicism had been nearly eliminated, in the minds of the middle colony Reformed another threat to the expansion of the Kingdom of God had not. Although the lot in England of the Dissenters was far better than that of the earlier Roundheads, the Arminianism of the established church as well as the general decline of religion and morality in the mother country horrified the middle colony Reformed. The attempts to tighten control over the colonies by the Crown-in-Parliament provoked the same sort of reaction from the middle colony Reformed as was generated in the Roundheads and the first Reformers by Catholicism. The Reformed clergy's fear of the imposition of Catholicism in sixteenth and seventeenth century Europe was transformed in the eighteenth century into fear of restriction of Reformed Protestantism's expansion.

As is true of every writer or thinker in any age, the middle colony Reformed preachers were not immune to the influences of their own culture. Not only those born into English-speaking families from the British Isles, but also even those from Dutch and German backgrounds evidenced knowledge of and allegiance to the historico-legal political tradition of freedoms and rights known to Britons. Under the press of the circumstances generated in the colonies by the British Acts, it is no wonder that many in the middle colonies cited their freedoms as free-born Britons to stimulate their fellow colonists to armed resistance. Thus, it may be speculated that this historico-legal tradition of certain freedoms and rights converged in the minds of the middle colony Reformed with their doctrine of the natural law of self-defense to produce an unintended natural *right* of self-defense, which might not have been a necessary product of their carefully developed Reformed theological system.

But the key to comprehending the distinctiveness of the middle colony revolutionary preaching is to see how the Reformed clergy handled their biblical theology. These ministers developed a kind of religious Manifest Destiny for America based on the biblical concept of the people of God. This religious Manifest Destiny was perhaps a natural transformation of earlier visions for America which took shape during the Great Awakening, but none of these Reformed ministers appear to have felt the tension that should have been created by the contrast between that ecclesiological hybrid and their most basic convictions concerning election and conversion.

The explanation of this lack of tension can be found in the dominant place of the covenant in their theology, as well as in the influence of the chosen nation ideology, a residue of the British belief. The covenant idea in English-speaking Puritanism comprehended not only individual salvation, but also the socio-political realm; only the Anabaptist sects rejected that comprehensiveness. When that kind of covenant was conflated with the chosen nation ideology, bequeathed to the colonies by British Protestantism in general, a potent ideological force was created, which, when adopted by one of the belligerents in an adversarial relationship, almost ineluctably led to resistance by combat.

To see the chosen nation idea at work in middle colony Reformed resistance preaching is also to find the Puritan ethos at work in a non-Puritan region. This research has indicated that a regionalism was present in middle colony resistance preaching, supporting those like Jerald Brauer who have questioned whether Puritanism is always an appropriate paradigm for early American historical studies. But this research also supports the conclusion that Puritanism's concept of God's chosen Protestant people was the driving force behind the fervor of Reformed ministers preaching revolution in the middle colonies.

In certain extraordinary mixtures of social pressures and dislocations and reactive political oppression, Reformed political ideology as expressed by the middle colony Reformed clergy, was pushed towards support for war and revolution and away from the normal, historical Reformed position of submission to governmental authorities. This development parallels the situation facing the British Puritans in the English civil wars of the 1640s.

Legitimation of "defensive" warfare by a chosen "Christian" nation, regardless of the motivations of its preachers, led to a number of results, some of which could not have been intended. First, it promoted among the masses the nascent nationalism of the American colonies. By extending the concept of the chosen people of God from New Englanders to all the colonists, it helped draw the belligerents together in "common cause against a common foe"[1] by means of a common identity. Second, without the elaborate covenant theology of New England Calvinism to give it boundaries, the idea that God had chosen America *as a nation* for special privileges and responsibilities weakened the idea that God had chosen *a particular group of individuals*—i.e., his church—for special blessings and responsibilities. It might not be too much to say with Mark Noll that "as a result of the war, American society in general replaced the church as the locus of communal Christian values."[2] Last, and much later historically, after secularization and perversion, the idea of a just war by a chosen "Christian" nation was exploited to promote an aggressive international imperialism; but by that time cultural power and influence had passed out of the hands of sincere, theologically controlled Reformed pastors, evangelists, and teachers, and into those of corporate boardrooms and political factions.

Notes

Chapter 1

1. William A. Mueller, *Church and State in Luther and Calvin* (Nashville, TN: Broadman Press, 1954), 53–56; J. Wayne Baker, *Heinrich Bullinger and the Covenant: the Other Reformed Tradition* (Athens, OH: Ohio University Press, 1980), 255, nt. 35; Quentin Skinner, *The Foundations of Modern Political Thought* (Cambridge: Cambridge University Press, 1978), 2:202, 205–6; Richard Gamble, "The Christian and the Tyrant: Beza and Knox on Political Resistance Theory," *Westminster Theological Journal* 46 (Spring 1984): 135; Richard Greaves, *Theology and Revolution in the Scottish Reformation* (Grand Rapids, MI: Christian University Press, 1980), 128–29; Theodore Beza, "The Right of Magistrates," in *Constitutionalism and Resistance in the Sixteenth Century*, edited and translated by Julian Franklin (New York: Pegasus Press, 1969), 108–9; *Vindiciae Contra Tyrannos*, edited by Harold Laski (Gloucester, MA: Peter Smith, 1963), 98–100; in *Christianity and Revolution, Radical Christian Testimonies, 1520–1650*, edited by Lowell Zuck (Philadelphia: Temple University Press, 1975), 137.

2. Jacques Courvoisier, *Zwingli, A Reformed Theologian* (Richmond, VA: John Knox Press, 1962), 84–85.

3. Esther Hildebrandt, "The Magdeburg Bekenntnis as a Possible Link between German and English Resistance Theories in the Sixteenth Century," *Archiv für Reformationsgeschichte* 71 (1981): 228–31. Quentin Skinner notes, however, that this kind of argument was found in Luther's earlier *Warning to his Dear German People*, in which Luther said that the ruler who exceeds the authority of his office had already reduced himself to the status of a private citizen and may be violently repelled in self-defense. Skinner, 2:202.

4. Quoted in Hildebrandt, 239.

5. Ibid., 239–40.

6. Dan Danner, "Resistance and the Ungodly Magistrate in the Sixteenth Century: the Marian Exiles," *Journal of the American Academy of Religion* 49 (September 1981): 471.

7. Baker 255, nt. 35; Skinner, 202; Courvoisier, 84–85; Greaves, 128–29; Richard Kyle, *The Mind of John Knox* (Lawrence, KS: Coronado Press, 1984), 252.

8. John Knox, *The Works of John Knox*, edited by David Laing, vol. 4 (Edinburgh: James Thin, 1895), 4:415–16.

9. Baker, 255, nt. 35.

10. Greaves, 128–29.

11. John Calvin, *Institutes of the Christian Religion*, translated by Ford Lewis Battles, edited by John T. McNeill, 2 vols. (Philadelphia: Westminster Press, 1960), 2:1518–19.

12. Quoted in John Milton, "Tenure of Kings and Magistrates," in *John Milton, Complete Poems and Major Prose*, edited with notes and introduction by Merritt Hughes (Indianapolis, IN: Odyssey Press, 1957), 775; see also Skinner's fine discussion, 230–33.

13. Skinner, 216. Skinner judges this line of reasoning to be merely a variant of secular "private law" arguments.

14. Courvoisier, 85.

15. Huldrych Zwingli, *Selected Writings of Huldrych Zwingli*, translated by E. J. Furcha (Allison Park, PA: Pickwick Publications, 1984), 1:279–80.

16. Hildebrandt, 228–31.

17. Skinner, 202.

18. Hildebrandt, 230–32.

19. Jungen holds that the politicizing of Calvinism began much earlier. The Lutheran *Bekenntnis . . . zu Mageburk* of 1550 was used as an example by Beza in his *De haereticis* and later in the actual title of his *Du Droit*. John Knox also cited the *Bekenntnis* in a debate before the Scottish General Assembly in 1564. Christoph Jungen, "Calvin and the Origin of Political Resistance Theory in the Calvinist Tradition" (Th.M. thesis, Westminster Theological Seminary, 1980), 183; Robert Kingdon, "The First Expression of Theodore Beza's Political Ideas," *Archiv für Reformationsgeschichte* 45 (1955), 92–93; Gamble, 134.

20. In Zuck, 137.

21. Ibid.

22. Hildebrandt, 236–37.

23. Skinner, 205–6.

24. David Wollman, "The Biblical Justification for Resistance to Authority in Ponet's and Goodman's Polemics," *Sixteenth Century Journal* 13 (1982): 32.

25. Ibid., 33–34.

26. John Ponet, *A Shorte Treatise of politike power, and of the true Obedience which subjects owe to kynges and other civil Governours* (1556; New York: Da Capo Press, 1972), 97–98. Hildebrandt observes that this was an original emphasis, not oriented towards religious issues; Hildebrandt, 244.

27. Ponet, 104–6.

28. Ibid., 233; cf. Skinner, 202–4.

29. Calvin, *Institutes*, 2:1518–19, nt. 54.

30. "Cependent le devoir du Magistrat inferieur est de maintenir, tant qu'il luy est possible, en son pays et sous sa jurisdiction la pureté di la religion; en quoy il faut qu'il procede avec grand prudence et bonne moderation, mais si faut-il qu'il y air aussi de la constance et magnanimité. Et de ceci la ville de Magdebourg a monstré de nostre temps un exemple bien notable . . . Ainsi donc, que plusiers Princes abusent de leur office, je di toutesfois que quiconque estime qu'il se faille deporter d'user de l'aide des Magistrat Chrestiens que Dieu presente, a l'encontre de la violence externe des infideles ou des heretiques, cestuy-la despouille l'Eglise de Dieu d'un secours merveilleusement utile ed mes nessaire. . . ." In Theodore Beza, *Du Droit des Magistrats*, edited by Robert Kingdon (Geneva: Librarie Droz, 1970), 69–70. On the other hand, Skinner argues that Beza eventually "ends up by withdrawing the inferior magistrates argument altogether." Skinner, 216.

31. Quoted in Beza, *Du Droit*, 73–75.

32. Beza, "The Right of Magistrates," in *Constitutionalism*, 108–9.

33. Ibid., 112.

34. Greaves, 133–34.

35. *Vindiciae*, 47, 71, 88.

36. George Sabine, *A History of Political Theory*, third ed. (New York: Holt, Rinehart, and Winston, 1961), 381.

37. *Vindiciae*, 98–110.

38. Hildebrandt, 245. However, since Goodman was perhaps more consciously Calvinistic than Ponet, this fact alone may merely be a result of Goodman's absorption of the Reformed tenet of *sola scriptura*.

39. Dan Danner, "Christopher Goodman and the English Protestant Tradition of Civil Disobedience," *Sixteenth Century Journal* 8 (1977): 63.

40. Danner, "Ungodly Magistrate," 475.

41. Hildebrandt, 243.

42. Ponet, 110–11. Ponet's arguments were apparently so convincing to the seventeenth century Puritans that they reprinted his book in 1639 and 1642. Wollman, 33.

43. Greaves, 127; Kyle, 252.

44. Knox, *Works*, 4:398.

45. Ibid., 4:415–16.

46. Ibid., 4:490.

47. Ibid., 4:501.

48. Greaves, 138; cf. Skinner, 237.

49. Knox, 4:505–6; cf. Skinner's comments, 235–38.

50. Knox, 4:527.

51. Ibid., 4:534.

52. Knox elaborated his resistance ideology in shorter statements. In his never-to-be-finished *Second Blast*, Knox said that no idolater or notorious sinner could ever become king of a Christian nation, and that no oath to such a one could ever be binding. If any such man was elected by the people and later manifested his true character, they might "moste justly . . . depose and punishe him." Ibid., 4:540.

53. Theodore Woolsey, "The Course of Instruction in Yale College," in *Yale College*, edited by William Kingsley (New York: Henry Holt and Co., 1879), 496–99. *The Creeds of Christendom*, edited by Philip Schaff, sixth ed., 3 vols. (Grand Rapids, MI: Baker Book House, 1983), 1:855–56. As an example of a particular Baptist patriotic minister and his Reformed theology, see Lee S. Johnson, "An Examination of the Role of John Gano in the Development of Baptist Life in North America, 1750–1804" (Ph.D. diss., Southwestern Baptist Theological Seminary), 94. Leonard Trinterud, *The Forming of an American Tradition* (Philadelphia: Westminster Press, 1949), 169–85; William Breitenbach, "The Consistent Calvinism of the New Divinity Movement," *William and Mary Quarterly*, third ser., 41 (April 1984), 241–47. Samuel Miller, *Memoir of the Rev. John Rodgers, D.D.* (1813; Philadelphia: Presbyterian Board of Publication, 1840), 223. Richard Greaves, "The Origins and Early Development of English Covenant Thought," *The Historian* 31 (November 1968), 29–33; John D. Eusden, introduction to *The Marrow of Theology*, by William Ames, translated and edited by John D. Eusden (1629; Durham, NC: Labyrinth Press, 1968), 19.

54. A. P. d'Entreves, *Natural Law, An Introduction to the Legal Philosophy* (London: Hutchinson University Library, 1931), 35.

55. Ibid., 33.

56. Ibid., 39–40. See also A. P. d'Entreves, introduction to *Aquinas, Selected Political Writings*, by Thomas Aquinas (New York: The Macmillan Co., 1959), xiii–xv. For an extended discussion of natural law and especially its transition from divine origin to an origin solely from human nature, see Heinrich Rommen, *The Natural Law* (New York: Arno Press, 1979), 70–109.

57. Verhey says that "Thomas's natural law claims to lead to the fulness of the good life minus only the theological virtues." Allen Verhey, "Natural Law in Aquinas and Calvin," in *God and the Good: Essays in Honor of Henry Stob*, edited by Clifton Orlebeke and Lewis Smedes (Grand Rapids, MI: Wm. B. Eerdmans, 1975), 82. As to how the Thomists applied natural law to resistance theory, see Skinner, 2:148–60.

58. Calvin, *Institutes*, 1:367–69, 2:1504–5; Zwingli, *Selected Writings*, 2:1–40; Henry Bullinger, *The Decades*, edited by Thomas Harding (1849; New York: Johnson Reprint Corp., 1968), 193, 211; *Vindiciae*, 80, 144–45, 180–81, 190–91, 225, 229; G. W. Williard, introduction, *Commentary on the Heidelberg Catechism*, by Zacharias Ursinus (1852; Phillipsburg, NJ: Presbyterian and Reformed Publishing Co., n.d.), 491–92; Johannes Wollebius, *Reformed Dogmatics*, edited by John W. Beardslee, III (Grand Rapids, MI: Baker Book House, 1977), 75–76; Heinrich Heppe, *Reformed Dogmatics Set Out and Illustrated from the Sources*, edited by Ernst Bizer, translated by G. T. Thomson (London: George Allen & Unwin, Ltd., 1950), 291–92; William

Ames, *Conscience with the Power and Cases Thereof* (1639; Amsterdam, NJ: Walter J. Johnson, Inc., 1975), 100; and William Ames, *The Marrow of Theology*, translated by John D. Eusden (1629; Philadelphia: Pilgrim's Press, 1968), 291; Samuel Rutherford, *Lex Rex, or the Law and the Prince* (1644; Harrisonburg, VA: Sprinkle Publications, 1982), 127, 162; Schaff, 3:640–41; Samuel Willard, *A Compleat Body of Divinity* (1726; New York: Johnson Reprint Corporation, 1969), 574.

59. Calvin, *Institutes*, 1:281–82; Schaff, 3:854–55; Ursinus, 491–92; Heppe, 291–92; Ames, *Conscience*, 100, 107; Schaff, 3:640–41, 652–53.

60. Calvin, *Institutes*, 1:281–82; Bullinger, *Decades*, 194–96, 206; Schaff, 3:588, 640–41, 652–53.

61. Calvin, *Institutes*, 1:47–48, 376–77; Zwingli, *Writings*, 2:52; Beza, "The Right of Magistrates," in *Constitutionalism*, 117; Ursinus, 491–92; Schaff, 3:588; Wollebius, 75–76; Ames, *Conscience*, 105–8.

62. Calvin, *Institutes*, 1:47–48, 376–77; Zwingli, *Writings*, 2:52; Ames, *Conscience*, 105–8.

63. Calvin, *Commentaries*, 98; *Institutes*, 1:283–84. Like all Reformed writers, though, the major emphasis of Calvin concerning natural law was in relation to salvation; see, for example, J. Peter Pelkonen, "The Teaching of John Calvin on the Nature and Function of the Conscience," *Lutheran Quarterly* 21 (February 1969): 74–88; Zwingli, *Writings*, 2:11–17; Beza, *Constitutionalism*, 106, 124–25; Ursinus, 612–13; Ernest Kevan, *The Grace of Law, A Study in Puritan Theology* (Grand Rapids, MI: Baker Book House, 1976), 74–76; Schaff, 3:588, 640–41, 652–53.

64. Calvin, *Institutes*, 1:355–62, 2:1503–4; Schaff, 3:907–8; Beza, *Constitutionalism*, 133.

65. Ursinus, 612–13.

66. Christopher Goodman, *How Superior Powers Ought to Be Obeyed* (1558; New York: Facsimile Text Society, 1931), 91–92, 158–59; Goodman's argumentation would seem to confirm Quentin Skinner's observation that, "With the earliest Calvinist revolutionaries, however, such allusions to natural law arguments had been little more than asides." Skinner, 320. The *Vindiciae Contra Tyrannos* from the same French Reformed Protestant resistance movement used more natural law arguments than did Goodman's tract, and it also equated natural law with the law of God. But since it is not at all certain whether it was written by a secular or an ecclesiastical figure, it is not of crucial importance for this chapter; cf. *Vindiciae.*

67. Ponet, 104–6.

68. Beza, *Constitutionalism*, 105–33, passim.

69. Schaff, 3:907–8; Beza, *Constitutionalism*, 133; Ursinus, 612–13.

70. John Platt, *Reformed Thought and Scholasticism* (Leiden: E. J. Brill, 1982), 179.

Chapter 2

1. Patrick Collinson, *English Puritanism*, General Series, no. 106 (London: The Historical Association, 1983), 31; Mary Fulbrook, *Piety & Politics* (Cambridge: Cambridge University Press, 1983), 128.

2. Timothy George, "War and Peace in the Puritan Tradition," *Church History* 53 (December 1984): 492–503.

3. Michael Finlayson, *Historians, Puritanism, and the English Revolution: the Religious Factor in English Politics Before and After the Interregnum* (Toronto: University of Toronto Press, 1983), 99–118; Nicholas Tyacke, "Puritanism, Arminianism, and Counter Revolution," in *Origins of the English Civil War,* edited by Conrad Russell (New York: Macmillan, 1973), 119–43, especially 138–43; Brian Manning, *The English People and the English Revolution, 1640–48* (London: Heinemann, 1976), 21–31.

4. Of course this was not peculiar to the Puritans; cf. J. Sears McGee, *The Godly Man in Stuart England* (New Haven, CT: Yale University Press, 1976), 144–52, for the Anglicans.

5. Against one kind of materialistic interpretation, see Christopher Hill, "Recent Interpretations of the Civil War," in *Puritanism and Revolution* (1958; New York: Schocken Books, 1967), 3–31. For a categorization of several kinds of materialistic interpretations, see Lawrence Stone, *The Causes of the English Revolution, 1529–1642* (London: Routledge & Kegan Paul, 1972), 3–25; especially 21–22, where he briefly touches on an "evil men" or "evil institutions" phase of revolutions in general. The concepts of the more radical groups involved in the civil war such as the Quakers or the Levelers will not be included.

6. Perry Miller, *The Puritans, A Sourcebook of Their Writings,* 2 vols., edited by Perry Miller and Thomas Johnson (New York: Harper & Row, 1963), 183–90.

7. John Owen, *A Sermon Preached to the Parliament, October 1652* (London, 1652), 50–52; Richard Vines, *Obedience to Magistrates, Both Supreme and Subordinate* (London, 1656), 11–12; Samuel Slater, "What is the Duty of Magistrates From the Highest to Lowest . . .?" *Puritan Sermons, 1659–1689,* 4 vols. (Wheaton, IL: Robert Owens Publishers, 1981), 488; Stephen Charnock, *The Complete Works of Stephen Charnock, B.D.,* 2 vols., edited by Thomas Smith (Edinburgh, 1864), 476; John Humfrey, *The Authority of the Magistrate* (London, 1672), 39; John Howe, *The Works of John Howe,* 2 vols. (London, n.d.), 2:934–35. This is directly comparable to what Aquinas and Calvin had already written.

8. John Owen, *A Sermon . . . With a Discourse about Toleration and the Duty of the Civil Magistrate about Religion* (London, January 31, 1649), 45; Slater, 489, 512; Charnock, 2:476; Humfrey, *Authority,* 39; Richard Baxter, cited in Richard Schlatter, *Richard Baxter and Puritan Politics* (New Brunswick, NJ: Rutgers University Press, 1957), 33.

9. Thomas Hill, *The Militant Church Triumphant Over the Dragon and His Angels* (London, 1643), 19; John Goodwin, *Anticavalierisme or, Truth Pleading As well the Necessity, as the Lawfulness of this Present War* (London, 1642), 2; John Ley, *The Fury of Warre* (London, 1643), 18–23; Stephen Lobb, *The Harmony Between the Old and Present Nonconformists Principles* (London, 1682), 55; John Corbet, *A Second Discourse of the Religion of England* (London, 1668), 43.

10. J. Goodwin, *Anticavalierisme,* 8–9; Stephen Marshall, *Of Resisting the Lawful Magistrate* (London, 1644), 27–28; Humfrey, *Authority,* 40; Howe, *Works,* 2:932.

11. J. Goodwin, *Anticavalierisme*, 7–8; Marshall quoted in Minne Weinstein, "Stephen Marshall and the Dilemma of the Political Puritan," *Journal of Presbyterian History* 46 (1968): 17.

12. J. Goodwin, *Anticavalierisme*, 7; Ames Short, *God Save the King* (London, 1660), 31–32; Slater, 482; John Humfrey, *Of Subjection to King George* (London, 1714), 10–13. This was written when Humfrey was ninety years old! William Hussey, *The Magistrates Charge for the Peoples Safetie* (London, 1647), 39–40; J. Goodwin, *Anticavalierisme*, 2. Presbyterian Richard Vines, during the Protectorate, while preaching on obedience to the magistrate, wisely avoided speaking directly to the question of the proper forms of government. He wrote, "I meddle not with that great question, agitated in this land in later years; which is in case when the Supremacy doth as it were fall a peeces within itself but with the duty of private Christians to the Magistrate, whether supream or subordinate . . . be subject to their Authoritie, for it is of God." Vines, 21–22.

13. Samuel Gibson, *The Ruine of the Authors and Fomentors of Civil Warre* (London, 1645), 12, 20; Owen, *Sermon*, 43; Hussey, 7; Howe, *Works*, 2:932. Humfrey, *Authority*, 40. The people were not, as one Elizabethan aristocrat deemed them, of "no account . . . but only to be ruled," even if many Puritans such as Richard Baxter did see property as requisite to political enfranchisement. Christopher Hill, *The Century of Revolution* (Walton-on-Thames: Thomas Nelson Sons, 1980), 37–38.

14. E.g., McGee, 124.

15. J. Goodwin, *Anticavalierisme*, 18.

16. Ibid., 8; Humfrey, *Authority*, 29, and *Subjection*, 6–7.

17. John Humfrey prior to 1680 argued that the end of government is not just the good of the people, but also "the honour of the Magistrate and the Glory of God." Humfrey, *Authority*, 75.

18. J. Goodwin, *Anticavalierisme*, 9–10. For example, Baptist John Tombes, one of Cromwell's "triers" in 1660 defended the supremacy of the restored king in both ecclesiastical and temporal things. But, "the King hath not power and authority to impose upon, or punish for neglect of things not agreeable to God's appointment in holy scripture . . . but he is to Govern by God's law, and to see in a political way that it is observed," Watts, 152n; John Toombes, *A Serious Consideration of the Oath of the King's Supremacy* (London, 1660), 19.

19. Miller, 183. As Richard Baxter wrote, "I appeal to Reason, whether to give men liberty to preach down Christ as a deceiver, to preach up Mohamet, to worship the Sun or Moon, to deny the Resurrection, or persuade men that there is no life but this, no Heaven or Hell, and to cry down Scripture and a holy life, and . . . etc." Even if the magistrate could not control the consciences of subjects, "yet they must force them to submit to holy doctrine, and learn the word of God, and to walk orderly and quietly in thatt condition, till they are brought to a voluntary profession of Christianity." Quoted in Schlatter, 33–35.

20. Owen; e.g., *Sermon*, 93, and *God's Work in Founding Zion and His Peoples Duty Thereupon* (Oxford, 1656), 36–41.

21. Owen, *Sermon*, 41, 78, 81.

22. *The Creeds of Christendom*, edited by Philip Schaff, sixth ed., 3 vols. (Grand Rapids, MI: Baker Book House, 1983), 3:513.

23. Ibid., 3:652.

24. Ley, 5–12.

25. Ibid., 12–15. Cf. Thomas Hill, 19–21, who also affirmed natural law as a possible legitimate basis for civil war being a just war.

26. Cf. Gibson, 13–14.

27. Ley, 15–17. The same texts were to be used by the eighteenth century middle colony Reformed to justify war against France and revolution against Britain.

28. John D. Eusden, *Puritans, Lawyers, and Politics in Early Seventeenth-Century England* (New Haven, CT: Yale University Press, 1958; repr., Archon Books, 1968), 133; Ernest Kevan, *The Grace of Law, A Study in Puritan Theology* (Grand Rapids, MI: Baker Book House, 1976), 54–55; Benjamin Wright, *American Interpretations of Natural Law* (Cambridge, MA: Harvard University Press, 1931), 15. Indeed, it was not until the middle of the eighteenth century that Congregational heirs of the Puritans would invert the primacy of Scripture over natural law: only then would they declare with Ebenezer Gay, "Revealed Religion is an *Additional* to Natural; built not on Ruins, but on the strong and everlasting Foundation of it." Ebenezer Gay, *Natural Religion, as Distinguish'd from Revealed* (Boston, 1759), 19–20. For a more complete discussion, see Robert J. Wilson, III, *The Benevolent Deity, Ebenezer Gay and the Rise of Rational Religion in New England, 1696–1787* (Philadelphia: University of Pennsylvania Press, 1984), 169–84.

29. Some Puritans went farther, as did John Preston, when he asserted in a quite un-Calvinistic passage: "There is in naturall man not only a light to know good . . . but there is even an Inclination in the will and affections, whereby men are provoked to doe good, and to oppose Evill. And therefore the proposition is true, that naturall men have some truths, because they have this Inclination remaining, even in the worst of them." Cited in Perry Miller, *Errand into the Wilderness* (New York: Harper & Row, 1956), 74–76.

30. William Ames, *The Marrow of Theology*, translated by John D. Eusden (1629; Philadelphia: Pilgrim's Press, 1968), 225–26.

31. Kevan, 74–76.

32. Samuel Rutherford, *Lex Rex, or the Law and the Prince* (1644; Harrisonburg, VA: Sprinkle Publications, 1982), 142.

33. Ibid., 97. Here Rutherford cited the earlier *Vindiciae*.

34. Ibid., 118–19.

35. William Ames, *Conscience with the Power and Cases Thereof* (1639; Amsterdam, NJ: Walter Johnson, Inc., 1975), 185–86, and *Marrow*, 317.

36. Sidney Ahlstrom, *A Religious History of the American People* (New Haven, CT: Yale University Press, 1972), 949.

37. *The Creeds*, 3:640–41, 652–53.

38. Wright, 45.

39. Cf. Harry Kerr, "The Election Sermon: Primer for Revolutionaries," *Speech Monographs* XXIX (March 1962): 13–22.

40. Jonathan Mitchell, *Nehemiah on the Wall in Troublesome Times* (Cambridge, MA, 1671), 11f.

41. Samuel Willard, *A Compleat Body of Divinity* (1726; New York: Johnson Reprint Corporation, 1969), 577.

42. Ibid., 568–69.

43. Ibid., 628–29.

44. John Wise, "Vindication of the Government of New-England Churches," in *The Puritans, A Sourcebook of Their Writings*, 2 vols., edited by Perry Miller and Thomas Johnson (New York: Harper & Row, 1963), 1:258.

45. John Barnard, *The Throne Established by Righteousness, A Sermon Preached Before his Excellency Jonathan Belcher, Esq.*, (Boston, 1734), 7.

46. Harry Stout, *The New England Soul* (New York: Oxford University Press, 1986), 297–98.

47. James Spalding, "Sermons Before Parliament (1640–49) as a Public Puritan Diary," *Church History* 36 (1967): 27.

48. John Wilson, *Pulpit in Parliament* (Princeton, NJ: Princeton University Press, 1969), 169. E.g., John Flavel, *The Works of John Flavel*, 6 vols. (London: Banner of Truth Trust, 1968), 4:313ff; John Owen, *The Works of John Owen, D.D.*, edited by William Goold (Edinburgh: T & T Clark, 1862), 9:3ff. Cf. John Bunyan, quoted in Christopher Hill, *Antichrist in Seventeenth-Century England* (London: Oxford University Press, 1971), 148.

49. Thomas M. Brown, "The Image of the Beast: Anti-Papal Rhetoric in Colonial America," in *Conspiracy: the Fear of Subversion in American History*, edited by Richard Curry and Thomas Brown (New York: Holt, Rinehart, and Winston, 1972), 3–11; *Puritans, The Millennium and the Future of Israel: Puritan Eschatology 1600–1660*, edited by Peter Toon (London: James Clarke & Co., Ltd., 1970), 21–32; *Creeds*, 3:658–59.

50. David Brady, *The Contribution of British Writers between 1560 and 1830 to the Interpretation of Revelation 13:16–18* (Tubingen: J.C.B. Mohr, 1983), 164, 178, 213; e.g. Owen, *Works*, 9:402; Flavel, 4:315f.

51. Bernard Capp, "Godly Rule and English Millennialism," *Past and Present* 52 (August 1971): 114; e.g., J. Goodwin, *Anticavalierisme*, 55–56, 65–72; Flavel, 4:315f. But during the Restoration decades such perceptions dimmed, for as DeJong notes in relation to missionary efforts, "eschatological expectations fueled and fanned missions into a bright blaze throughout the 1650's. At the Restoration much of the historical basis for those hopes disappeared. Significantly, the promotion of missions through the highly effective method of tracts virtually died out at the moment that the new king returned to England." J. A. DeJong, *As the Waters*

Cover the Sea, Millennial Expectations in the Rise of Anglo-American Missions, 1640–1810 (J. H. Kok N. V. Kampen, 1970), 78; cf. William Lamont, *Richard Baxter and the Millennium* (London: Croom Helm, 1979), 218.

52. Finlayson, 116–18.

53. Robin Clifton, "Fear of Popery," in *The Origins of the English Civil War*, edited by Conrad Russell (London: Macmillan, 1973), 150.

54. Finlayson, 99; cf. Wilson, 102–3.

55. Manning, 21–31.

56. How the Puritan clergy presented public affairs in terms of primary and secondary causes illustrates their ideological conservatism. For example, instead of holding the king accountable for his own oppressive actions, Edmund Calamy and Thomas Manton both declared that the sins of the nation had provoked God to unleash his judgment upon them in the form of civil war. Edmund Calamy, *England's Antidote Against the Plague of Civil Warre* (London, 1645), 2–5, 8–13; Thomas Manton, *Englands Spiritual Languishing* (London, 1641), 8ff.. The sins of idolatry, Sabbath breaking, profanity, sensuality, and self-seeking dominate the British Puritan lists of sins procuring God's judgment. Since these sins pervaded the elect British nation, it had to be chastised by a nation-wide calamity: Wilson, 180–89. This kind of national sin-guilt perspective helped divert the developing sensitivity of the British Puritans away from the injustices carried out by the king and his court toward the "malignants."

57. J. Goodwin, *Anticavalierisme*, 2; cf. Gibson, 20–22, 27; Hussey, 5; T. Hill, 21; Ley, 2; Philip Nye, *An Exhortation to the Taking of the Solemn League and Covenant* (London, 1644), 4; Cornelius Burges *et al.*, *A Vindication of the Ministers in and about London* (London, 1648), 3. Co-signers included Cornelius Burges, Edmund Calamy, William Gouge, Thomas Manton, and fifty-three other ministers. Bainton thinks it must have become very implausible in time: R. H. Bainton, "Congregationalism: From the Just War to the Crusade in the Puritan Revolution," *Andover Newton Theological School Bulletin*, Southworth Lecture, 35 (April 1943): 6. But McGee thinks that it was quite plausible; see page 133. At least one Puritan cited directives supposedly written by a Roman Catholic archbishop to the effect that all his agents were to set the Puritans against the established church; these directives the Puritan preacher tied to secret alliances of the Scots and the Irish and the Gun-Powder Plot; Ley, 19–21.

58. J. Goodwin, *Anticavalierisme*, 5, 12, 27.

59. Ibid., 11–16, 19–21.

60. T. Hill, 19–21.

61. Bainton, 6.

62. E.g., John Goodwin, who adopted earlier Calvinist resistance theories of Knox, Duplessis-Mornay, as well as more contemporary writers such as Milton and Rutherford. See his, *The Obstructors of Justice, A Defence of the Honourable Sentence passed upon the Late King by the High Court of Justice* (London: 1649), 46–47, 53, 71–72.

63. Capp, 114.

64. Stephen Marshall, *Meroz Cursed* (London, 1641), 8; T. Hill, 43; Gibson, 22, 25–27; Ley, 2, 18–19, 25, 40; J. Goodwin, *Anticavalierisme*, 2.

65. Even the feisty Independent John Goodwin, in 1642, argued that if a king commands something unlawful, of such a nature that a subject cannot "disobey it, but by a strong hand," he may take up arms to resist, "though not properly or directly against the King, yet against the command of the King." Even to Goodwin, those violently resisting must "conceive it to be just prerogative of the persons of Kings in what case soever, to be secure from the violence of men." Cf. Gibson 19–20; Bainton, 10. Surprisingly, the Calvinistic idea that inferior magistrates have the power to bring to account the supreme rulers of the land does not seem to have been of great importance in English Puritan resistance statements, except to radicals such as John Goodwin, when reproducing the arguments of the sixteenth century monarchomachists. This may have been so because the Calvinistic idea fit better the social situations found on the continent.

66. Williston Walker, *Creeds and Platforms of Congregationalism* (Philadelphia: Pilgrim Press, 1969), 393–94.

67. Stout, *New England Soul*, 6–7, 270–71; Jerald Brauer, "Puritanism, Revivalism, and the Revolution," in *Religion and the American Revolution*, edited by Jerald Brauer (Philadelphia: Fortress Press, 1976), 7–9; John Buchanan, "Puritan Philosophy of History from Restoration to Revolution," *Essex Institute Historical Collections* 104 (1968): 340–41.

68. Allen Carden, *Puritan Christianity in America* (Grand Rapids, MI: Baker Book House, 1990), 141.

69. Perry Miller, *Errand into the Wilderness* (New York: Harper & Row, 1964), 147–48.

70. T. H. Breen, *The Character of the Good Ruler, Puritan Political Ideas in New England, 1630–1730* (New York: W. W. Norton & Co., 1970), 37–38.

71. Miller, *Errand*, 147.

72. Breen, 110; cf. John Goodwin in old England, *Anticavalierisme*, 18.

73. Breen, 120–21.

74. Ibid., 213, 261.

75. Ibid., 152–53, 183.

76. Harry Stout, "The Puritans and Edwards," in *Jonathan Edwards and the American Experience*, edited by Nathan Hatch and Harry Stout (New York: Oxford University Press, 1988), 146–52; and Stout, *New England Soul*, 279.

77. Ibid., 295–96, 302.

78. Melvin Endy, Jr., "Just War, Holy War, and Millennialism in Revolutionary America," *William and Mary Quarterly*, third ser., 42 (January 1985): 11. For primary source examples, see the following in John Thornton's *Pulpit of the American Revolution* (New York: Burt Franklin, 1970): William Gordon, "A Discourse Preached . . . ," 204–5; Samuel Langdon, "A Sermon Preached . . . ," 235; and Samuel West, "A Sermon Preached . . . ," 284–87.

79. Brauer, 18–25; Patricia Bonomi, " 'A Just Opposition': The Great Awakening as a Radical Model," in *The Origins of Anglo-American Radicalism,* edited by Margaret Jacob and James Jacob (London: George Allen & Unwin, 1984), 243–56. Millennialism may have played a part in resistance ideology, but its role is controverted: see Stout, *New England Soul,* 306–9, and Melvin Endy as above.

80. Brauer, 12–18, 26–27.

81. Stout, *New England Soul,* 310.

Chapter 3

1. Alan Heimert, *Religion and the American Mind From the Great Awakening to the Revolutionary War* (Cambridge: Harvard University Press, 1966), 139; Perry Miller, *Errand into the Wilderness* (Cambridge: Belknap Press, a division of Harvard University Press, 1956; New York: Harper Torchbooks, Harper & Row, Publishers, 1964), 165–66; Harry Stout, "Religion, Communications, and the Ideological Origins of the American Revolution," *William and Mary Quarterly,* third ser., 34 (October 1977), 529ff; Patricia Bonomi, " 'A Just Opposition': The Great Awakening as a Radical Model," in *The Origins of Anglo-American Radicalism,* edited by Margaret Jacob and James Jacob (London: George Allen & Unwin, 1984), 243–56.

2. H. Shelton Smith, Robert Handy, and Lefferts Loetscher, *American Christianity, An Historical Interpretation with Representative Documents,* 2 vols. (New York: Charles Scribner's Sons, 1960), 17–18; Patricia Bonomi, " 'A Just Opposition,' " 245–48, 255–56n; Gregory Nobles, *Divisions Throughout the Whole, Politics and Society in Hampshire County, Massachusetts, 1740–1775* (Cambridge: Cambridge University Press, 1983), 39–46; Marilyn Westerkamp, *Triumph of the Laity, Scots-Irish Piety and the Great Awakening, 1625–1760* (New York: Oxford University Press, 1988), 183–94.

3. Lucy Bittinger, *The Germans in Colonial Times* (1901; New York: Russell & Russell, 1968), 242–43; Willard Dayton Brown, *A History of the Reformed Church in America* (New York: Board of Publication and Bible School Work, 1928), 76–77; H. Harbaugh, *The Fathers of the German Reformed Church,* second ed., 3 vols. (Lancaster, PA: J. M. Westhaeffer, 1872), 2:103; Leonard Kramer, "Muskets in the Pulpit: 1776–83," *Journal of Presbyterian History* 31 (December 1953): 229–30; Nelson Rightmyer, "Churches Under Enemy Occupation, Philadelphia, 1777–8," *Church History* 14 (1945): 48, 59.

4. Besides a significant number of Presbyterian published and manuscript documents, a relatively large number of Reformed MS sermons exist in several places in the middle Atlantic states. E.g., in the New York Public Library are about 150 sermons in French by Lewis Rou, a French Reformed pastor, dated from 1710 to 1750. A cache of Dutch-language sermons can be found at the Albany Institute of History and Art, McKinney Library, Albany, New York, containing many MS sermons of Eilardus Westerlo and Cornelius Van Sanvoort, none translated. Theodore Frelinghuysen in 1754 complained that no printers in his area of New York would print sermons in Dutch.

5. William W. Sweet, *Religion in Colonial America* (New York: Charles Scribner's Sons, 1942), 335.

6. Patricia Bonomi, *Under the Cope of Heaven, Religion, Society, and Politics in Colonial America* (New York: Oxford University Press, 1986), 220; Mark Noll, Nathan Hatch, and George Marsden, *The Search for Christian America* (Westchester, IL: Crossway Books, 1983), 53–54.

7. Edwin Gaustad, *Historical Atlas of Religion in America* (New York: Harper & Row, 1962), 167.

8. Carl Bridenbaugh, *Mitre and Sceptre, Transatlantic Faiths, Ideas, Personalities and Politics, 1689–1775* (New York: Oxford University Press, 1962), passim.

9. Nathan Hatch, "The Origins of Civil Millennialism in America," *William and Mary Quarterly*, third ser., 31 (July 1974): 407–30.

10. Alice Baldwin, *The New England Clergy and the American Revolution* (1928; repr., New York: Frederick Ungar Publishing Co., 1958), xi–xii.

11. George DeVries, Jr., "Church and State in New York, an Historical Account," *Reformed Journal* (November–December 1975): 18, passim. The Dutch Reformed churchmen probably had no fears of Anglican pressure since they held a special, protected status, at least in their New York stronghold. John Beardslee, III, "The Dutch Reformed Church and the American Revolution," *Journal of Presbyterian History* 54 (Spring 1976): 167.

12. Samuel Buell, MS sermon, "A thanksgiving upon the victory of his Royal Highness the Duke of Cumberland over the Pretendor in North Briton," dated 7–28–1746, in the Horace Scudder Collection, Washington University Library, Special Collections, St. Louis, MO.

13. John W. Thornton, *The Pulpit of the American Revolution* (Boston, 1860; repr., New York: Burt Franklin, 1970), 101.

14. Leonard Trinterud, *The Forming of an American Tradition* (Philadelphia: Westminster Press, 1949), 88.

15. Aaron Burr, *A Discourse delivered at New-Ark* (New York, 1755), 29.

16. Aaron Burr, *A Servant of God Dismissed from Labour to Rest, A Funeral Sermon* (New York, 1757), 14–19.

17. Robert Smith, *A Wheel in the Middle of a Wheel* (Philadelphia, 1759), 49–50.

18. E.g., H. S. Smith, Handy, and Loetscher, *American Christianity*, 1:276–80; or John Philip Boehm, *Life and Letters of the Rev. John Philip Boehm*, edited by William J. Hinke (New York: Arno Press, 1972), passim.

19. Henry Wm. Stoy, et al., "Address to the Honorable Robert Hunter Morris . . . from the Reformed Clergy . . . 1754," in *Minutes and Letters of the Coetus of the German Reformed Congregation in Pennsylvania, 1747–92* (Philadelphia: Reformed Church Publication Board, 1903), 120–21.

20. John Conrad Steiner, *Schuldigstes Leibes-und Ehren-Denkmahl* (Philadelphia: Miller, 1761), 30.

21. Theodorus Frelinghuysen, *Wars and Rumors of Wars, Heavens Decree over the World, A Sermon Preached in the Camp of the New-England Forces* (New York, 1755), 29.

22. Samuel Davies, *Sermons on Important Subjects*, fifth ed., 3 vols. (New York, 1792), 3:363.

23. Bridenbaugh, 114.

24. Francis Alison, MS sermon, "For a Thanksgiving on the Establishment of Peace, preached in Philadelphia, August the 9th, 1763," Presbyterian Historical Society, Philadelphia, PA. This sermon has been incorrectly identified, as handwriting analysis will show, by Leonard Kramer as having been written by Alison's protégé, John Ewing. See Kramer's "Presbyterians Approach the American Revolution," *Journal of Presbyterian History*, 31, no. 3 (September 1953): 172–73.

25. Francis Alison, typescript of manuscript sermon on Nehemiah 2:3–5, dated 7–27–1755, Presbyterian Historical Society, Philadelphia, PA.

26. Bridenbaugh, 130–68.

27. Hatch, 425. The importance of millennialism has recently been seriously challenged by Harry Stout, in his *The New England Soul* (New York: Oxford University Press, 1986), 306–9.

28. Buell, 1746 MS.

29. Gilbert Tennent, *The Late Association for Defense Encouraged, or the Lawfulness of a Defensive War* (Philadelphia, 1747), 6–7.

30. Ebenezer Prime, *The Importance of the Divine Presence with the Armies of God's People in their Martial Enterprize* (New York, 1759), 13.

31. Davies, *Sermons*, 3:398–404. This is contrary to the way Hatch, 420–21, misconstrues Davies's comments.

32. Smith, 55.

33. Alison, 1763 MS.

34. Frelinghuysen, *Wars*, 18, 27–28, 34, 36.

35. Christopher Beam, "Millennialism and American Nationalism, 1740–1800," *Journal of Presbyterian History* 54 (1976): 183.

36. Thomas Brown, "The Image of the Beast: Anti-Papal Rhetoric in Colonial America," in *Conspiracy: the Fear of Subversion in American History*, edited by Richard Curry and Thomas Brown (New York: Holt, Rinehart, and Winston, 1972), 14, 5.

37. Baldwin, *xii*; Bernard Bailyn also notes the extensive citations of leading seventeenth century secular thinkers such as Locke, Montesquieu, Grotius, and Pufendorf, but he also observes that the actual knowledge of them is at times superficial: *The Ideological Origins of the American Revolution* (Cambridge: Harvard University Press, 1967), 27–30.

38. Davies, *Sermons*, 3:391–94.

39. Ibid., 3:418.

40. Samuel Finley, *The Curse of Meroz, or the Danger of Neutrality in the Cause of God, and our Country* (Philadelphia, 1757), 22–26.

41. John Ewing, manuscript sermon on Matthew 5:5, dated 1761, Presbyterian Historical Society, Philadelphia, PA.

42. Frelinghuysen, *Wars*, 12–13, 19.

43. Tennent, *Association*, 10. Note the verbal similarity to Samuel Willard as discussed in the previous chapter on natural law in the Reformed tradition.

44. Ibid., 8.

45. Davies's longest sermons almost devoted to natural law had no political import: see his *Sermons*, 2:208ff and 3:216–30, and his *A Sermon on Man's Primitive State and the First Covenant* (Philadelphia: William Bradford, 1748).

46. But it may be that Alison's influence was not as great as McAllister would have it appear, at least among the ministerial ranks, for only three of his students from the New London Academy were later clergymen, as McAllister himself states, and it is not known whether one of them ministered in the middle colonies. Of his College of Philadelphia students, six were ordained to the ministry: Patrick Alison, Robert Davidson, William Hollingshead, James Latta, John King, and Thomas Reed. But of the middle colony Reformed clergy who have extant literary remains, only John Ewing is known to have studied under Alison; he later succeeded the latter at the College of Philadelphia. Since Witherspoon arrived in America after the period under consideration in this chapter, his influence was limited to those graduating from the College of New Jersey after 1768. But, even though Witherspoon satirically attacked Hutcheson in print, Caroline Robbins contends that he also is influenced to a great degree by Hutcheson. James McAllister, Jr., "Francis Alison and John Witherspoon: Political Philosophers and Revolutionaries," *Journal of Presbyterian History* 54 (Spring 1976): 35; Caroline Robbins, " 'When It Is That Colonies May Turn Independent': An Analysis of the Environment and Politics of Francis Hutcheson (1694–1746)," *William and Mary Quarterly*, third ser., 11 (April 1954): 218, 229–39 passim.

47. Gilbert Tennent, *The Happiness of Rewarding the Enemies of our Religion and Liberty* (Philadelphia: James Chattin, 1756), 8.

48. Davies, *Sermons*, 3:351, 2:202.

49. Tennent, *Association*, 18; cf. Finley, 10.

50. Chauncy Graham, *God Will Trouble the Troublers of His People* (New York, 1759), 21; note the verbal similarity to Finley, 10.

51. Prime, 52; Frelinghuysen, *Wars*, 12–13, 32–33.

52. Finley, 23–24; cf. Davies, *Sermons*, 3:375.

53. Davies, *Sermons*, 3:375.

54. Tennent, *Association*, 7.

55. Ewing, Matthew 5:5, MS. One unexpected result of this chapter's research is the absence of any essential difference between Old Side and New Side Presbyterians with regard to the Christian's role in society at war.

56. Ibid. Although the biblical texts of Judges 5:23 and Jeremiah 48:10 were favorites of Reformed preachers when preaching on war-related subjects, Ewing refrained from using them at this point.

57. John Berens, *Providence and Patriotism in Early America, 1640–1815* (Charlottesville, VA: University of Virginia Press, 1978).

58. Abraham Keteltas, *The Religious Soldier* (New York, 1759), 13–14.

59. George Duffield, "A Sermon on the Occasion of the Capture from the French of Fort Duquesne," *The Presbyterian Magazine* 8 (1858), 506–7. Cf. Prime, 15, and Frelinghuysen, *Wars*, 46. Duffield was a leading revivalist who finished his theological training with Robert Smith after graduating from the College of New Jersey in 1752 under Aaron Burr.

60. Alison, 1763 MS. Cf. Theodorus Frelinghuysen, *A Sermon Preached on the Occasion of the Late Treaty* (New York, 1754), 11–12.

61. Burr, *Discourse*, 27; Davies, *Sermons*, 3:406; Prime, 27; cf. John Buchanan, "Puritan Philosophy of History from the Restoration to Revolution," *Essex Institute Historical Collections* 104 (1968), 339–41. This perspective was a commonplace among Christians at that time, Congregational, Presbyterian, or Anglican.

62. Smith, 53.

63. Joseph Treat, *A Thanksgiving Sermon, occasioned by the Glorious News of the Reduction of the Havannah* (New York, 1762), 6; Burr, *Discourse*, 27; Prime, 47. Davies, for example, devotes more than seventy-eight lines of small typescript to such a sin list in *Sermons*, 3:380–82. The lists of procuring sins usually included luxury, profanity, Sabbath breaking, lying, greed, drunkenness, infidelity, whoredom, and effeminacy. "Luxury" in this period meant, according to the *Oxford English Dictionary*, lasciviousness or refined and intense enjoyment, indulgence in what is choice or costly in food, dress, or dwelling. This one sin, besides profanity, is found in all of the "sin lists" in the sermons examined here.

64. Finley, 10. In this perspective the middle colony Reformed were carrying on the doctrine of secondary causality, long an accepted part of Reformed doctrine— e.g., Westminster Confession V, 1–5—and its use by these preachers illustrates another tension in their thinking about taking up arms, similar to the tension related to using revelation and natural law to justify war. But its use in spite of the obvious tension shows how adherent those ministers were to their Reformed theological tradition.

65. Prime, 11; Frelinghuysen, *Wars*, 23.

66. Finley, 12.

67. Perry Miller, *Errand into the Wilderness* (Cambridge, MA: Belknap Press, a division of Harvard University Press, 1956; New York: Harper Torchbooks, Harper & Row, Publishers, 1964), 145–49.

68. Duffield, 509.

69. Davies, *Sermons*, 3:396–404.

70. This is perhaps an allusion to Jonathan Edwards's *History of the Work of Redemption*. See C. A. Patrides, *The Grand Design of God, the Literary Form of the Christian View of History* (London: Routledge & Kegan Paul, 1972), 119.

71. Keteltas, introduction.

72. Prime, title page.

73. Finley, 2–4.

74. Burr, *Servant*, title page, and *Discourse*, introduction.

75. That the sermon was probably the most powerful and pervasive means of transmission of ideas in the colonial period, see Stout, *New England Soul*, 3–5, but also see his caveat on 9–10 concerning the application of his results to areas outside of New England.

76. Trinterud, 180.

77. Richard Greaves, *Theology and Revolution in the Scottish Reformation* (Grand Rapids, MI: Christian University Press, a division of Wm. B. Eerdmans Publishing Co., 1980), 111–13.

78. Davies, *Sermons*, 3:374.

79. Prime, 1–9.

80. Burr, *Discourse*, 41.

81. Alison, 1763, MS.

82. Davies, *Sermons*, 3:352. The Presbyterian Church was first established on Long Island in the 1670s.

83. Finley, 27.

84. Frelinghuysen, *Wars*, 43.

85. Prime, 14.

86. Davies, *Sermons*, 3:351.

87. Smith, 49.

88. Edwin Gaustad, *Historical Atlas of Religion in America* (New York: Harper & Row, 1962), 167; but for more up-to-date numbers which would probably raise this kind of figure, see Patricia Bonomi and Peter Eisenstadt, "Church Adherence in the Eighteenth Century British American Colonies," *William and Mary Quarterly*, third ser., 39 (1982), 245–86, especially 273.

89. Ewing, Matthew 5:5, MS.

90. Tennent, *Association*, 38.

91. Davies, *Religion and Public Spirit*, 4–5.

92. Alan Heimert, *Religion and the American Mind from the Great Awakening to the Revolutionary War* (Cambridge: Harvard University Press, 1966), 66, 138, 142, 298.

93. Davies, *Sermons*, 2:239–40.

94. Tennent, *Association,* 38.

95. The view that millennialism pervaded, or even controlled, the political sermons of the New England clergy has been controverted also. Stout, *New England Soul,* 306–9.

Chapter 4

1. Caroline Robbins, *The Eighteenth-Century Commonwealthman* (Cambridge: Harvard University Press, 1959); Bernard Bailyn, *The Ideological Origins of the American Revolution* (Cambridge: Harvard University Press, 1967).

2. John Locke, *Two Treatises on Government,* revised edition, edited by Peter Laslett (New York: Cambridge University Press, 1960), 26; but note Locke's anomalous position as a republican in Robbins, 58–67. College of New Jersey (Woodbridge, NJ, 1760); Joe Kraus, "Book Collections of Five Colonial College Libraries" (Ph.D. diss., University of Illinois, 1960), 172–75; George Sensabaugh, *Milton in Early America* (Princeton, NJ: Princeton University Press, 1964), 34; Paul Spurlin, *Montesquieu in America, 1760–1801* (New York: Octagon Books, 1969), 51–64.

3. Bailyn, 45; Spurlin, 31–32, 88–89, 157–58; Caroline Robbins, "Algernon Sidney's Discourses Concerning Government: Textbook for Revolution," *William and Mary Quarterly,* third ser., 4 (1947), 270; Clinton Rossiter, *The Political Thought of the American Revolution* (1953; New York: Harcourt, Brace & World, Inc., 1963), 68.

4. Alice Baldwin, *The New England Clergy and the American Revolution* (1928; New York: Frederick Ungar, 1958), 11; Nathaniel Whitaker, "Antidote Against Toryism," *The Patriotic Preachers of the American Revolution,* edited by Frank Moore (New York: n.p., 1862); Harry Kerr, "The Election Sermon: Primer for Revolutionaries," *Speech Monographs* 29 (1962); Charles Van Tyne, "Influences of the Clergy, and of Religious and Sectarian Forces, on the American Revolution," *American Historical Review* 19 (1913); Sensabaugh, 54–66, 88nt., 127; Bailyn, 52; Baldwin, 10; Charles Akers, *Called unto Liberty, A Life of Jonathan Mayhew* (Cambridge, MA: Harvard University Press, 1964), 96; Baldwin, 95.

5. Except in reference to Locke's essay on religious tolerance in a personal letter to his cousin dated after the Revolution was well under way: John Henry Livingston, MS letter dated 2–28–1777, to Robert R. Livingston; Robert R. Livingston Papers, New York Public Library, New York.

6. Anna Haddow, *Political Science in American Colleges and Universities, 1636–1900* (New York: Octagon Books, 1969), 15.

7. Sensabaugh, 66. Perhaps the only link, an indirect one, is the citing of Milton in a few sermons of Samuel Davies (d. 1761) that was preached in Virginia and reprinted in Philadelphia. John Carmichael and Enoch Green were students of Davies at the College of New Jersey during his administration from 1759 to 1761, but neither Carmichael nor Green allude to Milton in their Revolutionary War sermons. European-trained Dutch Reformed pastor and fountainhead of the Great Awakening, Theodore Frelinghuysen does cite Milton's poetical works during the

French and Indian Wars: *Wars and Rumors of Wars, Heavens Decree Over the World, A Sermon Preached in the Camp of the New-England Forces* (New York, 1755).

8. Haddow, 14nt.

9. Norman Sykes, "Benjamin Hoadly, Bishop of Bangor," in *The Social and Political Ideas of Some English Thinkers of the Augustan Age* (New York: Barnes & Noble, 1928).

10. Kraus, 37–176 passim.

11. John Witherspoon, *Lectures on Moral Philosophy*, edited by Jack Scott (East Brunswick, NJ: Associated University Presses, 1982), 44.

12. Ibid., 189–91.

13. Andrew Hunter, MS, "Andrew Hunter's War Diary," Princeton University Library, Princeton, NJ.

14. Harry Stout, "Religion, Communications, and the Ideological Origins of the American Revolution," *William and Mary Quarterly*, third ser., 34 (1977), 540.

15. Martin Lodge, "The Crisis of the Church in the Middle Colonies, 1720–1750," *Pennsylvania Magazine of History and Biography* 95 (1971): 208.

16. *Documents of American History*, 2 vols., ninth edition, edited by Henry S. Commager (Englewood Cliffs, NJ: Prentice Hall, 1960), 61.

17. Henry Brackenridge, *Six Discourses Founded on the Scriptures* (Philadelphia: 1778), 83; Enoch Green, MS sermon, "upon his appointment as chaplain," dated 1776, Princeton University Library, Princeton University, Princeton, NJ; David Jones, *Defensive War* (Philadelphia, 1775), 14, 19; William Linn, *A Military Discourse* (Philadelphia, 1776), 12; Francis Alison, *et al.*, "An Address to the Ministers and Presbyterian Congregations in North Carolina," *Journal of Presbyterian History* 52 (1974), 391; John Witherspoon, *The Works of John Witherspoon*, 10 vols. (Edinburgh: Ogle & Aikman, 1804), 5:203.

18. James Armstrong, "Righteousness Exalteth a Nation" (1779), in *Light to My Path, Sermons by the Rev. James F. Armstrong, Revolutionary Chaplain*, edited by Marian McLeod (Trenton, NJ: First Presbyterian Church, 1976), 73; Enoch Green, MS sermon; Presbyterian Synod of New York and Philadelphia, *Records of the Presbyterian Church in the United States of America, 1706–1788* (New York: Arno Press, 1969), 467; William Tennent, III, *An Address, Occasioned by the Late Invasion* (Philadelphia: Bradford, 1774), 7–8.

19. John Adams, "Familiar Letters," *Journal of Presbyterian History* 52 (1974): 383, emphasis added.

20. Jones, 24; Robert Cooper, *Courage in a Good Cause* (Lancaster, PA: 1775), 23; William Foster, *True Fortitude Delineated* (Philadelphia: Dunlap, 1776), 11. Foster was Cooper's classmate at the College of New Jersey under Samuel Finley.

21. John Carmichael, *A Self-Defensive War Lawful* (Lancaster, PA: 1775), 88; Presbyterian Synod, 380; Alison, *et al.*, "Address," 389; Witherspoon, *Works*, 9:86; John Zubly, "The Law of Liberty" (1775), in *"A Warm & Zealous Spirit," John J. Zubly and the American Revolution, A Selection of His Writings*, edited by Randall Miller

(Macon, GA: Mercer University Press, 1982), 146; Jerrilyn Marston, "King and Congress: the Transfer of Political Legitimacy from the King to the Continental Congress, 1774–1776" (Ph.D. diss., Boston University, 1975), 109–23 passim. Carmichael studied under Samuel Davies at the College of New Jersey.

22. Matthew Wilson, "A Breviate of Scriptural Prophecies," *United States Magazine* (July 1779), 306. Wilson was a former student of leading Old Sider Francis Alison.

23. Hunter, MS diary.

24. Bailyn, 45–56.

25. Heinrich Rommen, *The Natural Law* (New York: Arno Press, 1979), 70–109.

26. Locke, 242–44, 314, 347.

27. Algernon Sidney, *Discourses Concerning Government*, third edition (London: A. Millar, 1751), 5–7, 29, 70.

28. Robbins, "Algernon," 281.

29. Sidney, 29.

30. Ernest Sirluck, "Milton's Political Thought: The First Cycle," *Modern Philology* 61 (February 1964): 209–10.

31. Jacob R. Hardenberg, MS commencement address at Queens College, "1774 file," Rutgers University Library, New Brunswick, NJ.

32. [Jacob Green], *Observations on the Reconciliation of Great-Britain and the Colonies* (Philadelphia, 1776), 9–10.

33. Cooper, 9.

34. Carmichael, 76.

35. Brackenridge, 35; Alison, *et al.*, "Address," 390; Cooper, 21; Foster, 11. Corollaries of the social compact, such as the consent of the governed and the lack of representation in Parliament, are also present in middle colony Calvinist sermons, but with no emphasis.

36. E.g., Locke, 374–77; John Milton, "The Tenure of Kings and Magistrates," in *John Milton, Complete Poems and Major Prose*, edited by Merritt Hughes (Indianapolis, IN: Odyssey Press, a division of Bobbs-Merrill Educational Publishing, 1957), 754, 802; Sidney, 23, 75–76.

37. Bailyn, 112–19.

38. Carmichael, 19; Cooper, 11.

39. Bailyn, 120.

40. Enoch Green, MS sermon.

41. J. Green, 10; Cooper, 21–22. One relevant manuscript I was unable to examine: Francis Alison, titled "Of the right of the Supreame Power," at the Presbyterian Historical Society, was referenced by Leonard Kramer in his 1947 Yale University Ph.D. dissertation, "The Political Ethics of the American Presbyterian Clergy in the Eighteenth Century," on page 406.

42. Jones, 12–13. This is the *salus populi*, reworded, but of the same substance as that of Puritan Independent John Goodwin of the previous century, and of Francis Hutcheson in the earlier eighteenth century. Cf. Caroline Robbins, " 'When It Is That Colonies May Turn Independent': An Analysis of the Environment and Politics of Francis Hutcheson (1694–1746)," *William and Mary Quarterly*, third ser., 11 (April 1954): 245.

43. Alison, *et al.*, "Address," 390. North Carolina was chosen because a large rural section was populated by Highland Scotch immigrants who had taken personal oaths of allegiance to George III. They had been pardoned by George II for their part on behalf of the pretender in the uprising of 1746–47 against the House of Hanover and were pardoned only on the condition that they migrate to the Carolinas.

44. Milton, "Tenure," 755.

45. Locke, 402–9.

46. Alison, *et al.*, "Address," 390.

47. Sidney, 376, 413.

48. Carmichael, 84; Cooper, 12; Jones, 13–14; Enoch Green, MS sermon; John Ewing, MS sermon on Matthew 5:5, Presbyterian Historical Society, Philadelphia, PA; James Miller, *Biographical Sketches and Sermons of Some of the First Ministers of the Associate Church in America* (Albany, NY: Hoffman and White, 1839), 35; Witherspoon, *Works*, 9:86.

49. Locke, 395–99; Milton, "Tenure," 755, 760; Sidney, 70.

50. Associate Presbytery, *Act of the Associate Presbytery in Pennsylvania for a Public Fast* (Philadelphia, 1774), 3–4; Brackenridge, 51; Cooper, 9; Linn, 9; Enoch Green, MS sermon; John Ewing, MS sermon on I Peter 5:6, Presbyterian Historical Society, Philadelphia; Israel Evans, *A Discourse Delivered at Easton* (Philadelphia, 1779), 4.

51. Locke, 446–49; Sidney, 130, 266–67; Milton, "Tenure," 755, 759–60.

52. Jones, 20, 24; Enoch Green, MS sermon; Carmichael, 22; Foster, 11; Presbyterian Synod, 380; Alison, *et al.*, "Address," 389–90.

53. Locke, 460–61, 467; Milton, "Tenure," 757, 763, 767.

54. Locke, 376–77.

55. Carmichael, 75.

56. Ewing, MS, Matthew 5:5.

57. Witherspoon, *Works*, 5:232–34.

58. Foster, 20.

59. Alison, *et al.*, "Address," 392. This position could be a continuation of Samuel Finley's 1757 harangue against neutral countrymen, *The Curse of Meroz*, for Finley was Foster's mentor at the College of New Jersey.

60. Locke, 465–66.

61. Milton, "Tenure," 779.

62. Cooper, 9, 22, 23, 27; Carmichael, 23; Tennent, III, 6–7; Presbyterian Synod, 380.

63. Alison, et al., "Address," 390–91.

64. Enoch Green, MS sermon.

65. E.g., Francis Alison, MS sermon, "For a Thanksgiving on the Establishment of Peace, preached in Philadelphia, August the 9th, 1763," Presbyterian Historical Society, Philadelphia.

66. The only substantial traceable connection is the influence of Francis Hutcheson via the teachings of Francis Alison and perhaps John Witherspoon. See Chapter 4.

Chapter 5

1. Phillip Schaff, *Creeds of Christendom* (1931), 3 vols., sixth edition (Grand Rapids, MI: Baker Book House, 1983), 3:640–41. Zacharias Ursinus, *The Commentary of Dr. Zacharias Ursinus on the Heidelberg Catechism*, translated by G. W. Williard (1852) (Phillipsburg, NJ: Presbyterian and Reformed Publishing Co., n.d.), 490–92.

2. E.g., William Foster, *True Fortitude Delineated* (Philadelphia: Dunlap, 1776), 4f; Laidlie, MS 6–21–1776.

3. Robert Cooper, *Courage in a Good Cause* (Lancaster, PA: 1775), 6; John Carmichael, *A Self-Defensive War Lawful* (Lancaster, PA: 1775), 13.

4. John Calvin, *Institutes of the Christian Religion*, 2 vols., translated by Ford Lewis Battles, edited by John T. McNeill (Philadelphia: Westminster Press, 1960), 1:367–68; but then there are those who suggest that Locke received his ideas of natural law from Calvinism, e.g., Winthrop Hudson, "John Locke—Preparing the Way for the Revolution," *Journal of the Presbyterian Historical Society* 42 (1964): 19–38.

5. Henry Brackenridge, *Six Discourses Founded on the Scriptures* (Philadelphia: 1778), 43; Carmichael, 13–15; Cooper, 12–13, 20, 27; Foster, 11; Enoch Green, MS sermon, "upon his appointment as chaplain," dated 1776, Princeton University Library, Princeton University, Princeton, NJ; David Jones, *Defensive War* (Philadelphia, 1775), 17; John Witherspoon, "Speech on Burgoyne's Surrender" (1777), in *Orations, From Homer to William McKinley*, edited by Mayo Hazeltine, vol. 5 (New York: Collier and Son, 1902), 2005.

6. Witherspoon, 2005.

7. Cooper, 4–13, passim.

8. Cf. Chapter 2; e.g., Carmichael, 13–15; Cooper, 27; Foster, 13. Foster was Cooper's classmate at the College of New Jersey under Samuel Finley.

9. Other examples implying Scripture was equivalent to natural law are in Carmichael, 77–79; Cooper, 27; and Foster, 13; Power, "Compend," TS of MS, Presbyterian Historical Society. However, the usage to which some middle colony Reformed ministers occasionally put natural law would seem today to be extremely tenuous; e.g., when Joseph Montgomery declared that it was legitimate for the colonists to conquer Indians who would not sell their land, for natural law

indicated that they were using the land far out of proportion for their native needs. Joseph Montgomery, *A Sermon, Preached at Christiana Bridge* (Philadelphia, 1775); 25 ftnt.

10. George Duffield, MS sermon dated 7–18–79, New York Public Library, New York; Foster, 17; Archibald Laidlie, MS sermon dated 6–21–1776, New-York Historical Society, New York; Robert Smith, *The Obligation of the Confederate States* (Philadelphia, 1782), 33.

11. Francis Alison, MS sermon, "For a Thanksgiving on the Establishment of Peace, preached in Philadelphia, August the 9th, 1763," Presbyterian Historical Society, Philadelphia; Cooper, 9; E. Green, '76 MS; Foster, 11; Archibald Laidlie, "L.D. XXXIX" MS; all interestingly use the word "exploded" to describe the passive obedience doctrine. Cf. Ewing, Matthew 5:5; Brackenridge, 24, 29, 37; Montgomery, 29.

12. Roland Bainton, *Christian Attitudes Toward War and Peace* (Nashville, TN: Abingdon, 1960), 89–146.

13. Archibald Laidlie, MS lecture on the Heidelberg Catechism, labeled "L(ord's) D(ay) XL," referring to questions #105, 106, and 107; held in the John Henry Livingston papers of the Albany branch of the New York State Library; dated 1767. Thus even though in the Livingston papers, it must be Laidlie, for, even though the script is similar, Livingston was in Europe that year earning his doctorate in theology.

14. John Ewing, MS sermon on Matthew 5:5, Presbyterian Historical Society, Philadelphia, delivered in Philadelphia in 1761 and 1767.

15. John Ewing, MS sermon on Matthew 5:10, Presbyterian Historical Society, Philadelphia, delivered in Philadelphia in 1766.

16. Enoch Green, MS entitled "Theological Responses," Princeton University Library, Princeton, NJ, c. 1757–60.

17. E.g., James Armstrong, "Righteousness Exalteth a Nation" (1779), in *Light to My Path, Sermons by the Rev. James F. Armstrong, Revolutionary Chaplain*, edited by Marian McLeod, Trenton, NJ: First Presbyterian Church, Trenton, 1976), 18; Presbyterian Synod of New York and Philadelphia, "Pastoral Letter" (1775), *Journal of Presbyterian History* 52 (1974): 380.

18. Ewing, Matthew 5:5.

19. H. Miller, 97f.

20. James Sproat, MS sermon on Psalm 137:1, preached in Philadelphia in July 1771 and August 1779, Rutgers University Library, New Brunswick, NJ.

21. Associate Presbytery, *Act of the Associate Presbytery in Pennsylvania for a Public Fast* (Philadelphia, 1774), 4.

22. William Tennent, III, *An Address, Occasioned by the Late Invasion* (Philadelphia, 1774), *iii*.

23. Ibid., 6–8.

24. Ibid., 9.

25. Minutes of the Dutchess Presbytery of New York, October 1774, MS, Presbyterian Historical Society, Philadelphia, PA.

26. H. Harbaugh, *The Fathers of the German Reformed Church*, second ed. (Lancaster, PA: J. M. Westhaeffer, 1872), 2:170.

27. Jobie Riley, "The Rhetoric of the German-Speaking Pulpit in Eighteenth-Century Pennsylvania," *Journal of the Lancaster County Historical Society* (Trinity, 1977), 157 nt. 18.

28. Oswald Seidensticker, *The First Century of German Printing in America, 1728–1830* (1893; New York: Kraus Reprint Corporation, 1966), 80–110.

29. Cooper, 10; Archibald Laidlie, MS lecture on the Heidelberg Catechism, labeled "L(ord's) D(ay) XXXIX," dated 1767, in the John Henry Livingston Papers of the New York State Library, Albany, New York.

30. Carmichael, 23–24.

31. Montgomery, 28.

32. Francis Alison *et al.*, "An Address to the Ministers and Presbyterian Congregations in North Carolina," *Journal of Presbyterian History* 52 (1974): 389.

33. Minutes of Dutchess, May 1775; John Maynard, *The Huguenot Church of New York, A History of the French Church of Saint Esprit* (New York: n.p., 1938), 202–3.

34. E. Green, MS sermon (1776).

35. William Smith, *Historical Memoirs from 12 July 1776 to 25 July 1778 of William Smith*, edited by William Sabine (New York: n.p., 1958), 182; Presbyterian Azel Roe in a MS sermon dated August of 1776, in the Presbyterian Historical Society archives, merely mentions, in a consistently pietistic manner, "Union to Christ, growing and increasing, is the grand only true Support of the Church of God at all times, and such are the Tryals of the present Day that it calls for a double portion of this Spirit . . . to endure Hardship in the Cause of Christ and have strength from the Lord to maintain it against all the Attacks of our Enemies"; see also for nonecclesiastical sources of the tenacious sentiment of loyalty to King George, Jerrilyn Marston, "King and Congress: the Transfer of Political Legitimacy from the King to the Continental Congress, 1774–1776" (Ph.D. diss., Boston University, 1975), 98ff.

36. Sproat, MS.

37. Tennent, 6.

38. Carmichael, 21.

39. Arthur Graeff, *The Relations Between the Pennsylvania Germans and the British Authorities (1750–1776)* (Norristown, PA: Norristown Herald, Inc., 1939), 232–35.

40. See previous chapter on British Puritan resistance ideology; cf. Marston, 148ff.

41. Carmichael, 23.

42. E.g., Henry Brackenridge, *Six Political Discourses Founded on the Scriptures* (Lancaster, PA, 1778), 83; Cooper, 21; George Duffield, MS sermon dated 7–18–1779,

New York Public Library, New York, NY; David Jones, *Defensive War* (Philadelphia, 1775), 14, 19; Evangelical Lutheran and Reformed Church Council, *Schreiben des Evangelisch-Lutherisch und Reformirten Kirchen-Raths . . . an die Teutschen Einwohner. . . .* (Philadelphia, 1775), 6; William Linn, *A Military Discourse* (Philadelphia, 1776), 12; Robert Smith, *The Obligation of the Confederate States* (Philadelphia, 1782), 3, 6; John Zubly, "The Law of Liberty" (Philadelphia, 1775), in *"A Warm & Zealous Spirit," John T. Zubly and the American Revolution,* edited by Randall Miller (Macon, GA: Mercer University Press, 1982), 125–29. This kind of attention given by the middle colony Reformed gives credence to James Smylie's contention concerning the meaning of the word "dominion" in the language of these preachers and theologians in his "Presbyterian Clergy and Problems of 'Dominion' in the Revolutionary Generation," *Journal of Presbyterian History* 48 (Fall 1970): 161–75.

43. Cooper, 20–21.

44. Montgomery, 26–27.

45. Foster, 11–12; cf. Montgomery, 26–27.

46. Presbyterian Synod, "Pastoral Letter," 380.

47. Associate Presbytery, *A Solemn Warning by the Associated Presbytery in Pennsylvania Addressed to all Persons into whose Hands it may come in these United States. . . .* (Lancaster, PA, 1778), 26; Brackenridge, 39; Wheeler Case, *Poems, Occasioned by Several Circumstances,* second ed. (New Haven, CT; also published in Philadelphia, 1778), 10; Israel Evans, *A Discourse, delivered at Easton* (Philadelphia, 1779), 4; Jacob Green, *A Sermon Delivered at Hanover . . .* (Chatham, PA, 1779), 4; Reformed Protestant Dutch Church, *Acts and Proceedings . . . 1771–1812* (New York: Board of Publication, 1859), 84; John Henry Livingston, MS sermon on Exodus 15:11–19, dated 12–18–1777, New Brunswick Seminary Library, New Brunswick, NJ; John Witherspoon, "The Dominion of Providence over the Passions of Men," in *The Works of John Witherspoon,* 10 vols. (Edinburgh, 1804), 5:202.

48. Carmichael, 24; Cooper, 11; John Ewing, MS sermon on I Peter 5:6 (1775), Presbyterian Historical Society, Philadelphia; E. Green, '76 MS; Jones, 16, 18, 23; Montgomery, 9, 27, 29; R. Smith, 4, 7.

49. Ewing, I Peter 5:6 MS; R. Smith, 7. Israel Evans, *A Discourse, Delivered on the 18th Day of December, 1777* (Lancaster, PA, 1778), 20–21.

50. Alexander MacWhorter, ". . . on British Brutality" (1777), in *New Jersey in the American Revolution,* edited by Larry Gerlach (Trenton, NJ: New Jersey Historical Commission, 1975), 296–97.

51. *Ecclesiastical Records, State of New York* (Albany, NY: J. B. Lyon Co., 1905), 6:4303–4.

52. Evangelical Lutheran and Reformed Church, 5. The consistently pietistic German Reformed Coetus or synod recorded in their official minutes and letters for the period 1774–81 only prayers for safety and lamentations because of religious declensions. The closest they came to any statement with significant political

content was a 1777 letter to the Church in their homeland in which they hoped
that God would make "our Fathers and brethren in Europe mediators and concilia-
tors between . . . Britain and America," *Minutes and Letters of the Coetus of the
German Reformed Congregation in Pennsylvania, 1747–92* (Philadelphia: Reformed
Church Publication Board, 1903), 365. There may yet be more pertinent sources
by German Reformed clergy in rather obscure locations, as indicated in Harbaugh,
Fathers, e.g., 2:82–83, 224–25, 286.

53. Evangelical Lutheran and Reformed Church, 8–10.

54. Ibid., 8–9.

55. Ibid., 7.

56. E.g., Cooper, 23; Ewing, I Peter MS; Foster, 11–12; Archibald Laidlie, MS sermon
    dated 5–21–1775, New-York Historical Society, New York, NY; Jones, 17–19.

Chapter 6

1. Francis Alison, MS sermon, "For a Thanksgiving on the Establishment of Peace,
   preached in Philadelphia, August the 9th, 1763," Presbyterian Historical Society,
   Philadelphia, PA; George Duffield, "Sermon on Isaiah 21:11–12" (1776), in *Courage in a Good Cause*, by George Duffield, Jr. (Philadelphia, 1861), 34–36 (this is,
   by analysis of the text, the full text of the MS sermon fragment now held in the
   Yale University Library); Armstrong, "The Lord was on our Side," in *Light to My
   Path, Sermons by the Rev. James F. Armstrong, Revolutionary Chaplain* (Trenton, NJ:
   1976), 21–22; John Ewing, MS sermon on Isaiah 8:12–14, dated 1781, Presbyterian Historical Society, Philadelphia.

2. E.g., William Foster, *True Fortitude Delineated* (Philadelphia: 1776), 4f; Archibald
   Laidlie, MS sermon dated 6–21–1776, Manuscript sermons; New Brunswick
   Theological Seminary, Gardner Sage Library, New Brunswick, NJ.

3. Armstrong, "The Lord was on our Side," 21; John Carmichael, *A Self-Defensive
   War Lawful* (Lancaster, PA: 1775), 21; Foster, 10; John Henry Livingston, MS
   sermon dated 12–18–77, New Brunswick Seminary.

4. Archibald Laidlie, MS sermon dated 3–6–76, New-York Historical Society, New
   York; John Witherspoon, "The Dominion of Providence over the Passions of
   Men," in *The Works of John Witherspoon*, 10 vols. (Edinburgh, 1804), 5:193–94;
   Israel Evans, *A Discourse, delivered at Easton* (Philadelphia: 1779), 4; John Henry
   Livingston, MS 12–18–77. E.g., George Duffield, MS sermon on Nehemiah 9:26,
   dated between 1775 and 1780 on internal evidence, New York Public Library,
   New York.

5. E.g., James Armstrong, "Righteousness Exalteth a Nation," in *Light to My Path,
   Sermons by the Rev. James F. Armstrong, Revolutionary Chaplain* (Trenton, NJ: 1976),
   13; Wheeler Case, *Poems, Occasioned by Several Circumstances*, second ed. (New
   Haven, CT: 1778), 20; Foster, 4, 10, 13, 20; Witherspoon, "Address to the Natives
   of Scotland Residing in America," *Works*, 5:233; all of which cite or allude to
   either Jeremiah 48:10 or Judges 5:23 or both and use those two passages to
   promote armed resistance in the same ways that Samuel Finley, president of the

College of New Jersey, 1761–66, during the French and Indian War, and as did Puritan divine Stephen Marshall in 1641 during the English civil wars.

6. Robert Cooper, *Courage in a Good Cause* (Lancaster, PA: 1775), 23; Francis Alison et al., *An Address to the Ministers and Presbyterian Congregations in North Carolina* (Philadelphia: 1775), 392. There were some Reformed ministers who preached toleration for those pacifists they deemed sincere, but even they anathematized and would condone no mercy for Tories: e.g., Carmichael, 17.

7. Cooper, 24; Laidlie, MSS sermons dated 5–17–75 and 3–5–76; David Jones, *Defensive War* (Philadelphia: 1775), 26.

8. God's providence and man's means are topics which recur in all discussions of the general theological issue of God's sovereignty or dominion. All these Calvinistic clergy were agreed that the perturbations of human history were under God's control, including wars and, as Francis Alison said in 1763, revolutions (Alison, MS sermon, 1763). But that general doctrine is transmuted in their war sermons into declarations about God's judgments in human history, and discussion of those sermons should be approached from that perspective.

9. Henry Hugh Brackenridge, *Six Discourses Founded on the Scriptures* (Philadelphia: 1778), 40; George Duffield, MS sermon dated 7–18–79, New York Public Library; John Henry Livingston, MS sermon on Proverbs 14 (c. 1775), New Brunswick Seminary Library; William Tennent, *An Address, Occasioned by the Late Invasion of the Liberties of the American Colonies by the British Parliament* (Philadelphia, 1774), 9.

10. George Duffield, Nehemiah 9:26 MS sermon, dated between 1775 and 1780, New York Public Library, New York, NY.

11. Livingston, MS sermon on Proverbs 14.

12. Foster, 12–20; Laidlie, New-York Historical Society MSS sermons dated 3–6–76, 4–19–76, 5–5–76; Livingston, New York Public Library MS dated 12–18–77.

13. E.g., Alison, MS sermon, 1763; Associate Presbytery, *A Solemn Warning by the Associated Presbytery in Pennsylvania Addressed to All Persons into whose Hands it may come in these United States . . .* (Lancaster, PA: 1778), 7–8, 14, 20–21, and Act 4; Jacob Green, *A Sermon Delivered at Hanover* (Chatham, PA: 1779), 5; Jones, 25; Laidlie, New-York Historical Society MSS 3–6–76, 3–10–76; James Sproat, MS sermon on Psalms 137:1, preached in Philadelphia in July 1771 and August 1779, Rutgers University Library, Special Collections, New Brunswick, NJ.

14. Alison, MS sermon, 1763; George Duffield, "Sermon on Isaiah 21:11–12," in *Courage in a Good Cause*, by George Duffield, Jr. (Philadelphia, 1861), 34; Evans, *Easton*, 4.

15. Joseph Montgomery, *A Sermon, Preached at Christiana Bridge* (Philadelphia, 1775), 24; Matthew Wilson, "A Breviate of Scriptural Prophecies," *United States Magazine* (July 1779): 304–5.

16. Case, *Poems*, 20; Duffield, "Isaiah 21," 34–36; Foster, 17; Robert Smith, *The Obligation of the Confederate States* (Philadelphia, 1782), 27–28 nt.; Wilson, 304–5.

17. Jacob R. Hardenberg, MS commencement address at Queens College, "1774 file," Rutgers University Library, New Brunswick, NJ; emphasis added.

18. John Henry Livingston, MS sermon on Exodus 15:11–19, dated 12–18–1777, New Brunswick Seminary Library, New Brunswick, NJ.

19. Foster, 16.

20. Ibid., 17; emphasis added.

21. Duffield, "Isaiah 21:11–12," 21, 34.

22. Ibid., 35.

23. Montgomery, 23–24.

24. Hardenberg, MS, several places; Armstrong, "our Side," 21; Cooper, 28; Enoch Green, MS sermon, "upon his appointment as chaplain," dated 1776, Princeton University Library, Princeton; Foster, 12, 19, 24; Jones, 20; Archibald Laidlie, New-York Historical Society, New York, MSS sermons dated 3–6–76, 5–17–76; Francis Alison et al., "An Address to the Ministers and Presbyterian Congregations in North Carolina," *Journal of Presbyterian History* 52 (Winter 1974): 391.

25. Montgomery, 29.

26. J. Green, *Hanover*, 5.

27. R. Smith, *Obligation*, 2.

28. Alison, MS sermon, 1763.

29. Laidlie, New-York Historical Society, MS sermon dated 3–6–76.

30. Duffield, "Isaiah 21," 34; [Jacob Green], *Observations on the Reconciliation of Great Britain and the colonies* (Philadelphia, 1776), 28–29.

31. Israel Evans, *A Discourse Delivered on the 18th Day of December, 1777* (Lancaster, PA, 1778), 6.

32. R. Smith, *Obligation*, 27–28 nt.

33. Nathan Hatch, "The Origins of Civil Millennialism in America: New England Clergymen, War with France, and the American Revolution," *William and Mary Quarterly*, third ser., XXXI (1974): 409.

34. Alison, MS sermon, 1763. Such sentiment can be found among English-speaking Protestants as far back as Hakluyt, who in 1584 saw the new land as the place where "Wee shall by plantinge there inlarge the glory of the gospell, and from England plante sincere religion, and provide a safe and a sure place to receive people from all parts of the worlde that are forced to flee for the truthe of Gods worde," as William W. Sweet records in his *Religion in Colonial America* (New York: Charles Scribner's Sons, 1942), 7.

35. Carmichael, 25.

36. Foster, 16; cf. Case's more poetic rendering of the same sentiment, 24.

37. Duffield, "Isaiah 21," 36–37; emphasis added.

38. Associate Presbytery, *Solemn Warning*, 26.

39. Ibid., 20.

40. Ibid., 27.

41. J. Green, *Hanover*, 22.

42. Evans, '79, 9. This was a widely accepted historical "truth." Cf. Theodorus Frelinghuysen, *Sermon Preached on the Occasion of the Late Treaty* (New York, 1754), 14; Witherspoon, "Dominion," *Works*, 5:202; and Jonathan Edwards, "The Latter Day is Probably to Begin in America," in *God's New Israel*, edited by Conrad Cherry, (Englewood Cliffs, NJ: Prentice-Hall, Inc., 1971), 58–59.

43. Wilson, 308.

44. Ibid., 303–6.

45. R. Smith, 27–28 footnote.

46. Ibid., 28 footnote.

47. Witherspoon, "Dominion," *Works*, 5:203; cf. Synod of New York and Philadelphia, "Pastoral letter," *Journal of Presbyterian History* 52 (1974): 381.

48. One exception to this was Henry Brackenridge's vehement attacks in his *Six Discourses Founded on the Scriptures* (Philadelphia, 1778), e.g., 50, 60, and 87. Brackenridge soon thereafter left the ministry for law.

49. Associate Presbytery, *Act of the Associate Presbytery in Pennsylvania for a Public Fast* (Philadelphia, 1774), 4; Evangelical Lutheran and Reformed, *Schreiben des Evangelisch-Lutherisch und Reformirten Kirchen-Raths . . . an die Teutschen Einwohner . . .* (Philadelphia, 1775), 10; Ewing, I Peter MS; Alison, *et al.*, *Address*, Philadelphia, 1775, 6.

50. John Zubly, "The Law of Liberty" (Philadelphia, 1775), in *"A Warm & Zealous Spirit," John T. Zubly and the American Revolution*, edited by Randall Miller (Macon, GA: Mercer University Press, 1982), 147.

51. Francis Alison, TS of MSS letters to Ezra Stiles dated 8–7–66 and 8–20–66, Presbyterian Historical Society, Philadelphia; Foster, 12; John Henry Livingston, MS letter to Robert Livingston dated 4–8–77, in Robert R. Livingston Papers, New York Public Library, New York; John Henry Livingston to Eilardus Westerlo, in Alexander Gunn, *Memoirs of the Rev. John Henry Livingston* (New York: Board of Publication of the Reformed Protestant Dutch Church, 1856), 155–56.

52. There is no hard evidence that the middle colony Reformed were influenced in any substantial way by the commonwealthmen, as has been shown by Bailyn and Akers for the New England patriot clergy, nor was there any reason for them to have been so. Their Reformed tradition along with classical English republican theorists already gave them all the necessary ingredients for a forceful resistance ideology.

Chapter 7

1. Max Savelle, "Nationalism and Other Loyalties in the American Revolution," *American Historical Review* 67 (July 1962): 917.

2. Mark Noll, *Christians in the American Revolution* (Washington, D.C.: Christian University Press, 1977), 167.

Bibliographic Essay

In general, neither the middle colonies nor their clergy have attracted the same amount of scholarly attention as have either the New England colonies or the South. Moreover, the few existing studies have lacked a guiding, established paradigm; Greenberg {Douglas Greenberg, "The Middle Colonies in Recent American Historiography," *William and Mary Quarterly*, third ser., 36 (1979)} indicts the "bewildering pluralism" of this region as having effectively prevented development of any dominant theme or motif, such as Puritanism in New England historiography. In particular, studies of middle colony religion have taken a back seat to political, economic, and social histories. Greenberg, in his extended bibliographic essay on middle colony research, found enough material for only two pages on religion (out of a total of thirty), and observed that Quaker studies have taken central place within that body of research {Jean Soderlund, *Quakers and Slavery, A Divided Spirit* (Princeton, NJ: Princeton University Press, 1985)}.

The small group of studies that do examine non-Quaker religious men and movements have rarely dealt with their ideas or theology. However, some work has been done on the history of the Great Awakening in the middle colonies and the institutional and ministerial problems associated with the revivals {e.g., Leonard Trinterud, *The Forming of an American Tradition* (Philadelphia: Westminster Press, 1949); Martin Lodge, "The Crisis of the Churches in the Middle Colonies, 1720–1750," *Pennsylvania Magazine of History and Biography* 95 (1971); James Tanis, *Dutch Calvinistic Pietism in the Middle Colonies: A Study of the Life and Theology of Theodorus Jacobus Frelinghuysen* (The Hague, 1967); Charles Maxson, *The Great Awakening in the Middle Colonies* (1929; Gloucester, MA: Peter Smith, 1958); and Patricia Bonomi, " 'Stewards of the Mysteries of God': Clerical Authority and the Great Awakening in the Middle Colonies," in *Professions and Professional Ideologies in America*, edited by Gerald Geison (Chapel Hill, NC: University of North Carolina Press, 1983)}. In addition, some investigators have addressed issues ancillary to the middle colony Reformed preaching of armed resistance, such as the ecclesiastical politics surrounding the origins of Reformed educational institutions, or church-state and religious freedom issues {Ann Gordon, "The College of Philadelphia, 1749–1779: Impact of an Institution" (Ph.D. diss., University of Wisconsin, 1975); Howard Miller, *The Revolutionary College, American Presbyterian Higher Education 1707–1837* (New York: New York University Press, 1976); George DeVries, Jr., "Church and State in New York: an Historical Account," *Reformed Journal* (December 1975); and Carl Bridenbaugh, *Mitre and Sceptre, Transatlantic Faiths, Ideas, Personalities and Politics, 1689–1775* (New York: Oxford University Press, 1962)}.

Several recent studies have treated well the patriotic activities of the middle colony Calvinist clergy. For example, Balmer, Beardslee, Kenney, Leiby, and Luidens {Randall Balmer, "Dutch Religion in an English World: Political Upheaval and Ethnic Conflict in the Middle Colonies" (Ph.D. diss., Princton University, 1985); John Beardslee, III, "The Reformed Church and the American Revolution," in *Piety and Patriotism: Bicentennial Studies of the Reformed Church in America, 1776–1976*, edited by James Van Hoeven (Grand Rapids, MI: Wm. B. Eerdmans, 1976); Alice Kenney, "The Albany Dutch, Loyalists and Patriots," *New York History* 42 (October 1961); Adrian Leiby, *The Revolutionary War in the Hackensack Valley* (New Brunswick, NJ: Rutgers University Press, 1980); John Luidens, "The Americanization of the Dutch Reformed Church" (Ph.D. diss., University of Oklahoma, 1969)} have substantially revised the filiopietistic myth that the Dutch Reformed church in the Revolution was, with the exception of a few individual Tory ministers and laymen, a united bloc of staunch patriots. Deep divisions existed within the Dutch Reformed on the question of armed revolution, especially in the "neutral ground" of the Hackensack Valley of New York. Unfortunately, the documents needed to analyze the theological motivations of Tory domines—sermons and lectures—are apparently nonexistent. Research on the Dutch Reformed clergy has shown that the Tory-patriot divisions correlate better with the Conferentie-Coetus schism of the pre-Revolutionary period than other factors researched to date.

John Smoot has traced the impact of the Revolutionary era Presbyterian on the formulation of the Pennsylvania state constitution {"Presbyterianism in Revolutionary Pennsylvania: Constitutionalism and Freedom" (Ph.D. diss., St. Mary's Seminary and University, 1982)}, though his short dissertation is weakened by an inadequate attention to primary sources. Christopher Beam and Alan Briceland {Christopher Beam, "Millennialism and American Nationalism, 1740–1800," *Journal of Presbyterian History* 54 (1976); Alan Briceland, "Daniel McCalla, 1748–1809: New Side Revolutionary and Jeffersonian," *Journal of Presbyterian History* 58 (Fall 1978)} include the patriotic support of Reverends Robert Smith and Daniel McCalla in biographical essays about two notable Presbyterian ministers, but they do not analyze any of their resistance ideology. Lee Johnson develops the same kind of treatment for one of the guiding lights of the early Baptists, John Gano {"An Examination of the Role of John Gano in the Development of Baptist Life in North America, 1750–1804" (Ph.D. diss., Southwestern Baptist Theological Seminary, 1986)}. Nelson Rightmyer, in an older article, provides a survey of the churches, and their ministers in Philadelphia, during the year of British occupation, but beyond indicating the general patriotic tenor of a few of the Reformed ministers' messages, does not reflect upon the actual content of those messages {"Churches Under Enemy Occupation, Philadelphia, 1777–8," *Church*

History 14 (1945)}. Finally, Charles Metzger's essay delineates the service of many chaplains in the Revolutionary armed forces {"Chaplains in the American Revolution," *Catholic Historical Review* 31 (1945)}; especially helpful is his table listing all the Revolutionary War chaplains, their denominations, and the units they served. But Metzger, like the preceding authors, does not discuss the political resistance ideology of his subjects.

While many works have examined or reinterpreted the patriotic activities, or the resistance preaching of the New England clergy in the Revolutionary period, only a small number have investigated the theology of the middle colony Calvinist clergy. None has done for the middle colonies what Alice Baldwin attempted to do for the New England patriot clergy: provide a theological analysis of the preaching of armed resistance by patriotic clergy {*The New England Clergy and the American Revolution* (New York: 1928)}. Such an analysis of the middle colony clergy is needed for four reasons: first, except for the pacifistic Quakers, the Reformed communions (Dutch Reformed, Presbyterian, Baptist, and German Reformed) accounted for the bulk of middle colony clergy; second, with the exception of one or two Presbyterian ministers and a handful of explicitly Tory Dutch domines, the Reformed clergy were overwhelmingly in the patriot camp; third, the Reformed were geographically concentrated in the middle colonies; fourth, the middle colony clergy of the Reformed churches prior to the end of the Revolution still adhered to the basic, orthodox Reformed faith—regardless of their views on revivals {Trinterud, 169–95}—unlike many of their New England counterparts.

One of the earlier, nonhagiographic studies of the theological underpinnings of colonial patriot preaching was C. Van Tyne's 1913 essay, "Influences of the Clergy, and of Religious and Sectarian Forces on the American Revolution" {*American Historical Review* 19 (1913)}. However, even though he addresses the middle colonies specifically, he footnotes only one middle colony minister in the Revolutionary period, William Smith, who, as an Anglican, favored reconciliation with Britain. Van Tyne only mentions the existence of the lengthy 1775 pamphlet from the German Lutheran and Reformed bodies in Philadelphia which urged support for Congress by the German-speaking population of New York and North Carolina. Alan Heimert, in his controversial *Religion and the American Mind* {Harvard University Press, 1966}, explicitly asserts the lack of middle colony primary sources as the reason for concentrating on New England, but the manner in which he argues the relative importance of Calvinistic revivalists in furthering revolutionary sentiment, compared to the Old Lights, might encourage the uncritical reader to extrapolate that conclusion to the middle colonies.

Christopher Beam's essay correlating the millennialism of eighteenth century Presbyterianism with the ascendant nationalism of the same period, also appears to analyze ministers of the middle colonies {"Millennialism and American Nationalism, 1740–1800," *Journal of Presbyterian History* 54 (1976)}. According to Beam, the eighteenth century Presbyterian ministers' "assertions of the notion of American mission were designed to convince their rebellious compatriots that their defiance of the Mother Country was in accord with God's plan for the redemption of the world," and indeed it would be natural for a complete military victory to influence the perceptions of even the Calvinistic clergy concerning their fledgling nation. However, Beam's article emphasizes Presbyterian ministerial statements made in the period *after* the Revolution; he references only two published middle colony sermons from the period 1758–82.

Four additional scholars focus on Presbyterian preachers' political thought in the latter eighteenth century: Mark Noll, James McAllister, Leonard Kramer, and Barbara Wingo. However, their studies are limited to single ministers, or narrowly focused periods of time. Noll's article on Jacob Green {"Observations on the Reconciliation of Politics and Religion in the Revolutionary New Jersey: the Case of Jacob Green," *Journal of Presbyterian History* 54 (1976)}, patriot pastor and political activist in New Jersey, concludes that natural law and natural rights philosophy formed the basis of Green's political resistance ideology; he does not attempt to analyze just how Green viewed natural law. McAllister convincingly demonstrates that Francis Alison and John Witherspoon, both preeminent Presbyterian divines and mentors of other Presbyterian leaders of that period, based their political thought on that of the Scottish moral philosopher Francis Hutcheson {"Francis Alison and John Witherspoon: Political Philosophers and Revolutionaries," *Journal of Presbyterian History* 54 (Spring 1976)}.

Leonard Kramer attempted to lay open the entire political ethic of the eighteenth century Presbyterian ministry, and his study necessarily emphasized the middle colony clergy {"The Political Ethics of the American Presbyterian Clergy in the Eighteenth Century" (Ph.D. diss., Yale University, 1942)}. However, while strong in theological analysis of the political sermons and tracts of revivalists Gilbert Tennent and Samuel Davies in the period 1745–63, Kramer's dissertation concentrated on clerical activities in the Revolutionary period. His analysis of their political ideology in the Revolutionary period is truncated. Kramer also attempted to analyze Witherspoon's and Alison's political-theological ethic, but he did not compare their ideas with the wartime messages of their former students. Rather, he seems content, for example, to point out the titles of graduation theses, the unnamed authors of which were, ostensibly, informed by Scottish commonsense philosophy. Milton Coalter's fine biography of Gilbert Tennent includes analysis of Tennent's political preaching, but as the subtitle indicates, its main focus is his part in the Great Awakening {*Gilbert Tennent, Son of Thunder* (New York: Greenwood Press, 1966)}.

Barbara Wingo's dissertation is more critical and well defined than Kramer's and focuses on the political ideology of the Presbyterian clergy in the period 1775–1808. Four men, she shows, were the primary formulators of the political theology of Presbyterians in the latter eighteenth century: John Witherspoon, Francis Alison, Charles Nisbet, and Samuel Stanhope Smith. All of these, she avers, adopted the moral philosophy of Francis Hutcheson of Scotland (Alison's mentor), though she allows that they added to their political ethic from other sources of thought, such as the Westminster Confession and Montesquieu {"Politics, Society, and Religion: The Presbyterian Clergy of Pennsylvania, New Jersey, and New York, and the Formation of the Nation, 1775–1808" (Ph.D. diss., Tulane University, 1976)}.

Such rigorous studies as Wingo's and McAllister's demonstrate that Alison and Witherspoon were greatly influenced by Hutcheson. There is also no doubt that those two intellectual giants influenced many young ministerial aspirants at the College of

Philadelphia and the College of New Jersey, where they taught for many years. Yet, the earliest manuscript evidence that Witherspoon lectured on moral philosophy at the College of New Jersey is dated 1772, and for Alison the earliest is 1759. Wingo conflates all Presbyterian writing in her period, beginning in 1775, and assumes they were all influenced by Hutcheson's philosophy. Her historiographical method is flawed by reading back into the earlier works of Presbyterian clergy, what was later the reigning philosophy in that denomination. Both Wingo and Kramer, by overemphasizing the indebtedness of Presbyterian political preachers to Witherspoon, miss Douglas Sloan's insight that "Before John Witherspoon, leaders of the New Side had viewed with suspicion certain central elements of Scottish Enlightenment thought" {*The Scottish Enlightenment and the American College Ideal* (New York: Teachers College Press, 1971)}.

While some of the preceding works attempted to analyze the political theology of the middle colony Presbyterian clergy, only rare attempts have been made to find the central issues behind the patriotic preaching of the Dutch Reformed clergy. In his dissertation on three Dutch Reformed patriotic clergymen {"The Application of Holy Things: A Study of the Covenant Preaching in the Eighteenth Century Dutch Colonial Church" (Ph.D. diss., Westminster Theological Seminary, 1985)}, Jack Klunder examined scores of their sermons, both published and manuscript, and concluded that the concept of covenant formed the overall core of their preaching. While he did not examine the sermons for their political content, his annotated bibliography of sermons in the New Brunswick Seminary Library does locate those that are politically oriented, though they are few in number. Of slightly more relevance to an analysis of the political ideology of patriotic Dutch Reformed preaching is Earl Kennedy's article on Linn, Livingston, and Laidlie {"From Providence to Civil Religion: Some 'Dutch' Reformed Interpretations of America in the Revolutionary Era," *Reformed Review* 29 (1976)}. Although Kennedy directly quotes from some of their patriotic, Revolutionary War sermons, since his purpose is to deal with the millennialism of their thought, the analysis of those sermons is slightly skewed. Most of his focus, at least for Linn and Livingston, is on the post-Revolutionary period. Moreover, the large corpus of very readable manuscript sermons of Laidlie in the New York Public Library and those of Livingston in the Albany branch of the New York State Library, were not examined by Kennedy.

Laidlie, Livingston, and Linn will continue to attract the interest of religious historians of this period because their writings are mostly in English. However, as Beardslee has pointed out, these three men were not truly ethnic Dutch domines and, because of their relationship with Presbyterianism, might not be typical of the Dutch Reformed patriot preachers. Any substantial conclusions concerning either ethnic Dutch Reformed patriot clergy or the fewer Tory Dutch ministers, in terms of their resistance ideology, must await translation and editing of the eighteenth century Dutch-language manuscript collections in the archives of New York, New Jersey, and Pennsylvania. Similarly, although some work has been done on the German Reformed and Baptist ministers' activities during the Revolution (mostly hagiographic), no analysis can be found as to what kind of resistance ideology they preached, if any.

Richard Pointer's substantial *Protestant Pluralism and the New York Experience* not only comprehends within its scope the activities of all the denominations present in New York in the eighteenth century, but it also points out salient features of Reformed preaching during the Revolutionary period. For example, he notes that early in the Revolutionary period the high degree of political pluralism in the Protestant churches led to ministerial avoidance of politicizing sermons. While he is especially strong in analyzing the alliances of the sundry Protestant groups with either the Tories or patriots, he only touches upon the ideology of resistance. He accomplishes his intent: to explain the effect of religious pluralism upon New York society.

Three studies that surpass those sketched above in insight and relevance are John Berens's revisionist *Providence and Patriotism in Early America* {Charlottesville, VA: University of Virginia Press, 1978}, James Smylie's article "Presbyterian Clergy and Problems of 'Dominion' in the Revolutionary Generation" {*Journal of Presbyterian History* 48 (1970)}, and Melvin Endy's prize-winning essay "Just War, Holy War, and Millennialism in Revolutionary America" {*William and Mary Quarterly*, third ser., 42 (1985)}. All three worked with primary Reformed sources from the middle colony ministers' Revolutionary resistance sermons and tracts; they were concerned with the theological infrastructure of those sermons and tracts; and, they followed proper historiographic method. Berens demonstrates persuasively that a providential mind-set—a theological worldview—held the allegiance throughout the eighteenth century of nearly all intellectual leaders, a proposition that contradicts historians who would maintain that the Enlightenment gained intellectual hegemony in that era. He also establishes that one of the primary motivations for patriot preachers in the Revolutionary period was the belief that one of "the ultimate reasons why Divine Providence was guiding and supporting America" in her struggle for liberty was that she was to be an "asylum" for the oppressed, even more, that she was to have a hand in cosmic redemption. Although Berens claims to "have read every surviving sermon and oration delivered on a communal or national occasion in America between 1763 and 1789," yet, the greatest portion of these "more than 850 pieces" of literature are from New England. On the other hand, the citations he does give from middle colony Reformed clergy do fit, as it were, his conclusions, and must be considered carefully in any analysis of middle colony Calvinist clergy resistance ideology. Smylie shows that the word "dominion" held a distinctly different connotation to the Presbyterian clergy than it did for Bernard Bailyn's secular New England revolutionaries who operated under the influence of the commonwealthmen. To the Presbyterian clergy, "dominion" was primarily *God's* rule of the world. Although Smylie also concentrates perhaps too much attention on Witherspoon, his insight is a helpful warning not to assume that those clerics were overwhelmed by ideological Whiggery in their political statements.

Melvin Endy brings the discussion about clerical resistance preaching back to basics by reexamining a number of interpretations of clerical resistance preaching in the Revolutionary era. Endy argues that those such as Bercovitch, Hatch, and Royster, who contend that the resistance preachers saw the Revolution as more of a holy war than simply a just war, are inaccurate because they have overemphasized a few selected sources or focused on just one of the "holy war criteria." After estimating that, at most, only one-sixth of the sermons and tracts published during the Revolution (from a sample of 190 pieces) "placed the nation in the context of millennial history," he concludes:

> The essential characteristic of a holy war is the belligerents' conviction that they are playing an indispensable role in a struggle that must be won if the ultimate goal of history is to be achieved. Only a minority of the American clerics had such a grandiose regard for their provincial outposts, and most of those who did entertain such thoughts were hesitating and tentative.

Selected Bibliography

1. Primary Sources

a. Unpublished documents

Alison, Francis. MS sermon, "For a Thanksgiving on the Establishment of Peace, preached in Philadelphia, August the 9th, 1763." Presbyterian Historical Society, Philadelphia, PA.

————. Typescripts of MS letters to Ezra Stiles, dated 8–7–1766 and 8–20–1766. Presbyterian Historical Society, Philadelphia, PA.

————. Typescript of manuscript sermon on Nehemiah 2:3–5, dated 7–27–1755, Presbyterian Historical Society, Philadelphia, PA.

Buell, Samuel. MS sermon, "A thanksgiving upon the victory of his Royal Highness the Duke of Cumberland over the Pretendor in North Briton," dated 7–28–1746, in the Horace Scudder Collection, Washington University Library, Special Collections, St. Louis, MO.

Caldwell, James. MS letter to M. Geary, dated 10–6–1778, in the Ely Papers of the New Jersey Historical Society, Newark, NJ.

Duffield, George. Manuscript sermons 1775–80. Rare Books and Manuscripts Division, New York Public Library, NY.

————. Manuscript sermon on Nehemiah 9:26, dated between 1775 and 1780 on internal evidence, Rare Books and Manuscripts Division, New York Public Library.

Dutchess Presbytery. Minutes of the Dutchess Presbytery of New York, 1774–1776, Manuscript, Presbyterian Historical Society, Philadelphia, PA.

Ewing, John. Manuscript sermons on Matthew 5:5 (1772); Matthew 5:10 (1771); I Peter 5:6 (1775); and Isaiah 8:12–14 (1781). Presbyterian Historical Society, Philadelphia, PA.

Green, Enoch. Manuscript sermon, "upon his appointment as chaplain of the New Jersey militia." Dated 1776. Princeton University Library, Department of Rare Books and Special Collections, Princeton, NJ.

—————. Manuscript notebook entitled "Theological Responses" (c. 1760), Princeton University Library, Department of Rare Books and Special Collections, Princeton, NJ.

Hardenberg, Jacob R. MS commencement address at Queens College, "1774 file," Rutgers University Library, Special Collections and Archives, New Brunswick, NJ.

Hunter, Andrew. Manuscript, "Andrew Hunter's War Diary," Princeton University Library, Rare Books and Special Collections, Princeton, NJ.

Laidlie, Archibald. Miscellaneous manuscript sermons, including those on the Heidelberg Catechism. New-York Historical Society, New York, NY.

—————. Manuscript sermons, 1763–79. New Brunswick Theological Seminary, Gardner Sage Library. New Brunswick, NJ.

—————. Manuscript sermon dated 7–18–1779, New York Public Library, Rare Books and Manuscripts Division, NY.

—————. Manuscript lectures on the Heidelberg Catechism, labeled "L(ord's) D(ay) XXXIX" and "L(ord's) D(ay) XL," referring to questions nos. 105, 106, and 107; held in the John Henry Livingston Papers of the Albany branch of the New York State Library; dated 1767.

Livingston, John Henry. Manuscript letters to Robert R. Livingston, Chancellor of New York. Robert R. Livingston Papers, New York Public Library, Rare Books and Manuscripts Division, NY. Dated 2–28 and 4–8–1777.

—————. Manuscript sermons 1775–80. New Brunswick Theological Seminary, Gardner Sage Library. New Brunswick, NJ.

Power, James. Typescript of manuscript entitled "A Compend of Theology, by James Power, a Candidate for the Ministry, under the care of the Newcastle Presbytery," dated 3–13–1768. Presbyterian Historical Society, Philadelphia, PA.

Roe, Azel. MS sermon "God blesseth the Provisions of Grace to His Church." Dated 8–1776. Presbyterian Historical Society, Philadelphia, PA.

Sproat, James. Manuscript sermon on Psalms 137:1, preached in Philadelphia in 7–1771 and 8–1779. Rutgers University Library, Special Collections and Archives, New Brunswick, NJ.

b. Published documents

Adams, John. "Familiar Letters," *Journal of Presbyterian History* 52 (1974): 383.

Alison, Francis; Ewing, John; Rodgers, John; Treat, Joseph. "Minutes of the General Convention of Delegates, 1766 to 1775." *Journal of Presbyterian History* 52 (Winter 1974): 339–43.

Alison, Francis; Sproat, James; Duffield, George; Davidson, Robert. "An Address to the Ministers and Presbyterian Congregations in North Carolina." *Journal of Presbyterian History* 52 (Winter 1974): 388–92.

Alison, Francis; Sproat, James; Duffield, George; Davidson, Robert. *An Address to the Ministers and Presbyterian Congregations in North Carolina.* Philadelphia, 1775.

Ames, William. *Conscience with the Power and Cases Thereof.* 1639; reprint, Amsterdam, NJ: Walter J. Johnson, Inc., 1975.

———. *The Marrow of Theology.* Translated with introduction by John D. Eusden. Philadelphia: Pilgrim's Press, 1968.

Armstrong, James. "Righteousness Exalteth a Nation" (1779). In *Light to My Path, Sermons by the Rev. James F. Armstrong, Revolutionary Chaplain.* Edited by Marian McLeod. Trenton, NJ: First Presbyterian Church, 1976.

———. "The Lord was on our Side" (1781). In *Light to My Path, Sermons by the Rev. James F. Armstrong, Revolutionary Chaplain.* Edited by Marian McLeod. Trenton, NJ: First Presbyterian Church, 1976.

Associate Presbytery. *Act of the Associate Presbytery in Pennsylvania for a Public Fast.* Philadelphia, 1774.

———. *A Solemn Warning by the Associated Presbytery in Pennsylvania Addressed to all Persons into whose Hands it may come in these United States. . . .* Lancaster, PA, 1778.

Barnard, John. *The Throne Established by Righteousness, A Sermon Preached Before his Excellency Jonathan Belcher, Esq.* Boston, 1734.

Beza, Theodore. "The Right of Magistrates." In *Constitutionalism and Resistance in the Sixteenth Century.* Edited and translated by Julian Franklin. New York: Pegasus, 1969.

———. *Du Droit des Magistrats.* Edited by Robert Kingdon. Geneva: Librarie Droz, 1970.

Boehm, John Philip. *Life and Letters of the Rev. John Philip Boehm,* Edited by William J. Hinke. New York: Arno Press, 1972.

Brackenridge, Henry Hugh. *Six Discourses Founded on the Scriptures.* Philadelphia, 1778.

Bullinger, Henry. *The Decades.* Edited by Thomas Harding. 1849; reprint, New York: Johnson Reprint Corp., 1968.

Burr, Aaron. *A Discourse delivered at New-Ark.* New York, 1755.

———. *A Servant of God Dismissed from Labour to Rest, A Funeral Sermon.* New York, 1757.

Calamy, Edward. *England's Antidote Against the Plague of Civil Warre.* London, 1645.

Calvin, John. *Commentaries on the Epistle of Paul the Apostle to the Romans.* Edited and translated by John Owen. 1849; Grand Rapids, MI: William B. Eerdmans, 1948.

———. *Institutes of the Christian Religion.* 2 vols. Translated by Ford Lewis Battles. Edited by John T. McNeill. Philadelphia, Westminster Press: 1960.

Carmichael, John. *A Self-Defensive War Lawful. Proved in a sermon preached at Lancaster before Captain Ross's Company of Militia June 4, 1775.* Lancaster, PA, 1775.

Case, Wheeler. *Poems, Occasioned by Several Circumstances.* second ed. New Haven, CT, 1778. (Multiple editions in New Haven, New York, and Philadelphia were printed.)

Charnock, Stephen. *The Complete Works of Stephen Charnock, B.D.* 2 vols. Introduction by Reverend James McCosh. Edinburgh: James Nichol, 1864.

Cooper, Robert. *Courage in a Good Cause, A sermon preached near Shippenburgh, the 31st of August, 1775.* Lancaster, PA, 1775.

Corbet, John. *A Second Discourse of the Religion of England.* London, 1668.

Davies, Samuel. *A Sermon on Man's Primitive State and the First Covenant.* Philadelphia: William Bradford, 1748.

———. *Sermons on Important Subjects.* Fifth ed. 3 vols. New York: T. Allen, 1792.

Documents of American History. Ninth ed. 2 vols. Edited by Henry S. Commager. Englewood Cliffs, NJ: Prentice Hall, 1960.

Duffield, George. "Sermon on Isaiah 21:11–12." Preached 3–17–1776 at the Pine Street Presbyterian Church, Philadelphia. In *Courage in a Good Cause: or the Lawful and Courageous Use of the Sword.* By George Duffield, Jr. Philadelphia, 1861. (This is, by analysis of the text, the full text of the manuscript sermon fragment now held in the Yale University Library.)

———. "A Sermon on the Occasion of the Capture from the French of Fort Duquesne," *The Presbyterian Magazine* 8 (1858): 506–7.

Ecclesiastical Records, State of New York. 7 vols. Albany, NY: J. B. Lyon Co., 1901–1916.

Evangelical Lutheran and Reformed Church Council. *Schreiben des Evangelisch-Lutherisch und Reformirten Kirchen-Raths. . . an die Teutschen Einwohner . . . .* Philadelphia, 1775.

Evans, Israel. *A Discourse, delivered at Easton.* Philadelphia, 1779.

———. *A Discourse Delivered Near York.* Philadelphia, 1782.

———. *A Discourse, Delivered on the 18th Day of December, 1777.* Lancaster, PA, 1778.

Ferguson, Robert. *Whether the Preserving the Protestant Religion was the Motive unto, or the End, that was designed in the Late Revolution.* London, 1695.

Finley, Samuel. *The Curse of Meroz, or the Danger of Neutrality in the Cause of God, and our Country.* Philadelphia, 1757.

Flavel, John. *The Works of John Flavel.* Vols. 4 and 6. London: Banner of Truth Trust, 1968.

Foster, William. *True Fortitude Delineated.* Philadelphia, 1776.

Frelinghuysen, Theodorus. *Wars and Rumors of Wars, Heavens Decree Over the World, A Sermon Preached in the Camp of the New-England Forces.* New York, 1755.

———. *A Sermon Preached on the Occasion of the Late Treaty.* New York, 1754.

German Reformed Church. *Minutes and Letters of the Coetus of the German Reformed Congregation in Pennsylvania, 1747–92.* Philadelphia: Reformed Church Publication Board, 1903.

Gibson, Samuel. *The Ruine of the Authors and Fomentors of Civil Warre.* London, 1645.

Goodman, Christopher. *How Superior Powers Ought to be Obeyed.* 1558. New York: Facsimile Text Society, 1931.

Goodwin, John. *AntiCavalierisme or, Truth Pleading As well the Necessity, as the Lawfulness of this Present War.* London, 1642.

Goodwin, Thomas. "A Glimpse of Sions Glory." In *The Works of Thomas Goodwin, D.D.* General preface by John C. Miller. Vol. 12, Sermons and Notes of Sermons. Edinburgh: James Nichol, 1861.

Graham, Chauncy. *God Will Trouble the Troublers of His People.* New York, 1759.

[Green, Jacob]. *Observations on the Reconciliation of Great Britain and the colonies.* Philadelphia, 1776.

―――. *A Sermon Delivered at Hanover . . . April 22d, 1778.* Chatham, PA, 1779.

Heppe, Heinrich. *Reformed Dogmatics Set Out and Illustrated from the Sources.* Translated by G. T. Thomson. Edited by Ernst Bizer. London: George Allen & Unwin, Ltd., 1950.

Hill, Thomas. *The Militant Church Triumphant Over the Dragon and His Angels.* London, 1643.

Howe, John. *A Discourse Relating to the Much Lamented Death and Solemn Funeral of . . . Queen Mary.* London, 1695.

―――. *The Works of John Howe.* Vol. 2. London, n.p., n.d.

Humfrey, John. *The Authority of the Magistrate.* London, 1672.

―――. *Of Subjection to King George. A Brief Essay for Reconciling Whigs and Tories and Abolishing all Distinctions.* London, 1714.

Hussey, William. *The Magistrates Charge for the Peoples Safetie.* London, 1647.

Jones, David. *Defensive War.* Philadelphia, 1775.

Keteltas, Abraham. *The Religious Soldier.* New York, 1759.

Knox, John. *The Works of John Knox.* Vol. 4. Edited by David Laing. Edinburgh: James Thin, 1895.

Ley, John. *The Fury of Warre.* London, 1643.

Linn, William. *A Military Discourse.* Philadelphia, 1776.

Livingston, John Henry. Letter (no. 58) to George Clinton, dated 5–23–1775. In *The Public Papers of George Clinton, First Governor of New York.* Vol. 1, Military. New York: Wynkoop Hallenbeck Crawford Co., 1899.

Lobb, Stephen. *The Harmony Between the Old and Present Nonconformists Principles.* London, 1682.

―――. *The True Dissenter.* London, 1685.

Locke, John. *Two Treatises on Government.* Revised edition. Edited by Peter Laslett. New York: Cambridge University Press, 1960.

MacWhorter, Alexander. ". . . on British Brutality" (1777). In *New Jersey in the American Revolution.* Edited by Larry Gerlach. Trenton, NJ: New Jersey Historical Commission, 1975.

Manton, Thomas. *Englands Spiritual Languishing.* London, 1648.

Marshall, Stephen. *Meroz Cursed.* London, 1641.

————. *Of Resisting the Lawful Magistrate.* London, 1644.

Miller, James. *Biographical Sketches and Sermons of Some of the First Ministers of the Associate Church in America.* Albany, NY: Hoffman and White, 1839.

Milton, John. "The Tenure of Kings and Magistrates." In *John Milton, Complete Poems and Major Prose.* Edited by Merritt Hughes. Indianapolis, IN: Odyssey Press, a division of Bobbs-Merrill Educational Publishing, 1957.

Mitchell, Jonathan. *Nehemiah on the Wall in Troublesome Times.* Cambridge, MA, 1671.

Montgomery, Joseph. *A Sermon, Preached at Christiana Bridge.* Philadelphia, 1775.

Owen, John. *A Sermon Preached to the Parliament, October, 1652.* London, 1652.

————. *The Works of John Owen, D.D.* Vols. 8, 9, and 13. Edited by Reverend William Goold. Edinburgh: T & T Clark, 1862.

Ponet, John. *A Shorte Treatise of politike power, and of the true Obedience which subjects owe to kynges and other civil Governours.* 1556. New York: Da Capo Press, 1972.

Presbyterian Synod of New York and Philadelphia. *Records of the Presbyterian Church in the United States of America, 1706–1788.* New York: Arno Press, 1969.

————. "Pastoral Letter." 1775. *Journal of Presbyterian History* 52 (1974): 378–82.

Prime, Ebenezer. *The Importance of the Divine Presence with the Armies of God's People in their Martial Enterprize.* New York, 1759.

Reformed Protestant Dutch Church. *Acts and Proceedings of the General Synod of the Reformed Protestant Dutch Church in North America.* Vol. 1, 1771–1812. New York: Board of Publication of the RPDC, 1859.

Rutherford, Samuel. *Lex Rex, or the Law and the Prince.* 1644; Harrisonburg, VA: Sprinkle Publications, 1982.

Short, Ames. *God Save the King.* London, 1660.

Sidney, Algernon. *Discourses Concerning Government.* Third edition. London: A. Millar, 1751.

Slater, Samuel. "What is the Duty of Magistrates From the Highest to Lowest, for the Suppressing of Profaness?" In *Puritan Sermons, 1659–1689.* Vol. 4. Wheaton, IL: Robert Owens Publishers, 1981.

Smith, Robert. *The Obligation of the Confederate States.* Philadelphia, 1782.

————. *A Wheel in the Middle of a Wheel.* Philadelphia, 1759.

Smith, William. *Historical Memoirs, From 12 July 1776 to 25 July 1778 of William Smith.* Edited by William Sabine. New York: n.p., 1958.

Steiner, John Conrad. *Schuldigstes Leibes-und Ehren-Denkmahl.* Philadelphia: Miller, 1761.

Stoy, Henry Wm. and others. "Address to the Honorable Robert Hunter Morris . . . from the Reformed Clergy . . . 1754." In *Minutes and Letters of the Coetus of the German Reformed Congregation in Pennsylvania, 1747–92.* Philadelphia: Reformed Church Publication Board, 1903.

Tennent, Gilbert. *The Happiness of Rewarding the Enemies of our Religion and Liberty.* Philadelphia: James Chattin, 1756.

————. *The Late Association for Defense Encouraged, or the Lawfulness of a Defensive War.* Philadelphia, 1747.

Tennent, William, III. *An Address, Occasioned by the Late Invasion of the Liberties of the American Colonies by the British Parliament.* Philadelphia, 1774.

Thornton, John W. *The Pulpit of the American Revolution.* Boston, 1860; reprint, New York: Burt Franklin, 1970.

Tombes, John. *Saints No Smiters, or Smiting Civil Powers Not the Work of Saints Being a Treatise Shewing the Doctrine and Attempts of Quinto-Monarchians or Fifth Monarchy Men About Smiting Powers to be damnable and Anti-Christian.* London, 1664.

Treat, Joseph. *A Thanksgiving Sermon, occasioned by the Glorious News of the Reduction of the Havannah.* New York, 1762.

Ursinus, Zacharias. *The Commentary of Dr. Zacharias Ursinus on the Heidelberg Catechism.* Translated by G. W. Williard. 1852; reprint Phillipsburg, NJ: Presbyterian and Reformed Publishing Co., n.d.

Vindiciae Contra Tyrannos. Edited by Harold Laski. Gloucester, MA: Peter Smith, 1963.

Vines, Richard. *Obedience to Magistrates, Both Supreme and Subordinate.* London, 1656.

Willard, Samuel. *A Compleat Body of Divinity.* 1726; reprint, New York: Johnson Reprint Corporation, 1969.

Wilson, Matthew. "A Breviate of Scriptural Prophecies," *United States Magazine* (July 1779): 299–308.

Wise, John. "Vindication of the Government of New-England Churches." In *The Puritans, A Sourcebook of Their Writings.* Vol. 1. Edited by Perry Miller and Thomas Johnson. New York: Harper & Row, 1963: 257–69.

Witherspoon, John. *Lectures on Moral Philosophy.* Edited by Jack Scott. East Brunswick, NJ: Associated University Presses, 1982.

————. "Speech on Burgoyne's Surrender." 1777. In *Orations, From Homer to William McKinley.* Vol. 5. Edited by Mayo Hazeltine. New York: Collier and Son, 1902.

————. *The Works of John Witherspoon,* 10 vols. Edinburgh: Ogle & Aikman, 1804.

Wollebius, Johannes. *Reformed Dogmatics.* Edited by John W. Beardslee, III. Grand Rapids, MI: Baker Book House, 1977.

Zubly, John. "The Law of Liberty" (Philadelphia, 1775). In *"A Warm & Zealous Spirit," John T. Zubly and the American Revolution.* Edited by Randall Miller. Macon, GA: Mercer University Press, 1982.

Zuck, Lowell, ed. *Christianity and Revolution, Radical Christian Testimonies, 1520–1650.* Philadelphia: Temple University Press, 1975.

Zwingli, Ulrich. *Selected Writings of Huldrych Zwingli.* 2 vols. Translated by E. J. Furcha. Allison Park, PA: Pickwick Publications, 1984.

————. *On Providence and other essays*. Edited for Samuel Macauley Jackson by William J. Hinke. 1922; Durham, NC: Labyrinth Press, 1983.

2. Secondary Sources

a. Books

Abernathy, George. *The English Presbyterians and the Stuart Restoration, 1648–1663*. Philadelphia: Transactions of the American Philosophical Society, New Series, Vol. 55, part 2, 1965.

Akers, Charles. *Called unto Liberty, A Life of Jonathan Mayhew*. Cambridge: Harvard University Press, 1964.

Bailyn, Bernard. *The Ideological Origins of the American Revolution*. Cambridge: Harvard University Press, 1967.

Bainton, Roland. *Christian Attitudes Toward War and Peace*. Nashville, TN: Abingdon, 1960.

Baker, J. Wayne. *Heinrich Bullinger and the Covenant*. Athens, OH: Ohio University Press, 1980.

Baldwin, Alice. *The New England Clergy and the American Revolution*. 1928; reprint, New York: Frederick Ungar Publishing Co., 1958.

Berens, John. *Providence and Patriotism in Early America, 1640–1815*. Charlottesville, VA: University of Virginia Press, 1978.

Bittinger, Lucy. *The Germans in Colonial Times*. 1901; reprint, New York: Russell & Russell, 1968.

Bonomi, Patricia. *Under the Cope of Heaven, Religion, Society, and Politics in Colonial America*. New York: Oxford University Press, 1986.

Brady, David. *The Contribution of British Writers between 1560 and 1830 to the Interpretation of Revelation 13:16–18*. Tubingen: J.C.B. Mohr, 1983.

Breen, T. H. *The Character of the Good Ruler, Puritan Political Ideas in New England, 1630–1730*. New York: W. W. Norton & Co., 1970.

Bridenbaugh, Carl. *Mitre and Sceptre, Transatlantic Faiths, Ideas, Personalities and Politics, 1689–1775*. New York: Oxford University Press, 1962.

Brown, Willard Dayton. *A History of the Reformed Church in America*. New York: Board of Publication and Bible School Work, 1928.

Carden, Allen. *Puritan Christianity in America*. Grand Rapids, MI: Baker Book House, 1990.

Coalter, Milton. *Gilbert Tennent, Son of Thunder*. New York: Greenwood Press, 1966.

Collinson, Patrick. *English Puritanism*. General Series, no. 106 of The Historical Association, London (1983), 31.

Courvoisier, Jacques. *Zwingli, A Reformed Theologian*. Richmond, VA: John Knox Press, 1962.

Cremeans, Charles. *The Reception of Calvinist Thought in England.* Urbana, IL: University of Illinois Press, 1949.

Davidson, Philip. *Propaganda and the American Revolution.* Chapel Hill, NC: University of North Carolina Press, 1941.

DeJong, J. A. *As the Waters Cover the Sea, Millennial Expectations in the Rise of Anglo-American Missions, 1640–1810.* J. H. Kok N. V. Kampen, 1970.

Finlayson, Michael. *Historians, Puritanism, and the English Revolution: the Religious Factor in English Politics before and after the Interregnum.* Toronto: University of Toronto Press, 1983.

Firth, Katharine. *The Apocalyptic Tradition in Reformation Britain, 1530–1645.* London: Oxford University, 1922.

Fulbrook, Mary. *Piety & Politics.* Cambridge: Cambridge University Press, 1983.

Gaustad, Edwin. *Historical Atlas of Religion in America.* New York: Harper & Row, 1962.

Graeff, Arthur. *The Relations Between the Pennsylvania Germans and the British Authorities (1750–1776).* Norristown, PA: Norristown Herald, Inc., 1939.

Greaves, Richard. *Theology and Revolution in the Scottish Reformation.* Grand Rapids, MI: Christian University Press, 1980.

Gunn, Alexander. *Memoirs of the Rev. John Henry Livingston.* New York: Board of Publication of the Reformed Protestant Dutch Church, 1856.

Harbaugh, H. *The Fathers of the German Reformed Church.* Second ed. 3 vols. Lancaster, PA: J. M. Westhaeffer, 1872.

Heimert, Alan. *Religion and the American Mind: From the Great Awakening to the Revolutionary War.* Cambridge: Harvard University Press, 1966.

Hill, Christopher. *Antichrist in Seventeenth-Century England.* London: Oxford University Press, 1971.

————. *The Century of Revolution.* Walton-on-Thames: Thomas Nelson Sons, 1980.

Kyle, Richard. *The Mind of John Knox.* Lawrence, KS: Coronado Press, 1984.

Lacey, D. R. *Dissent and Parliamentary Politics in England, 1661–1689.* New Brunswick, NJ: Rutgers University Press, 1969.

Lamont, William. *Richard Baxter and the Millennium.* London: Croom Helm, 1979.

Leiby, Adrian. *The Revolutionary War in the Hackensack Valley, the Jersey Dutch and the Neutral Ground, 1775–1783.* New Brunswick, NJ: Rutgers University Press, 1980.

Manning, Brian. *The English People and the English Revolution, 1640–48.* London: Heinemann, 1976.

Maxson, Charles. *The Great Awakening in the Middle Colonies.* 1929; Gloucester, MA: Peter Smith, 1958.

Maynard, John. *The Huguenot Church of New York, A History of the French Church of Saint Esprit.* New York: n.p., 1938.

McGee, J. Sears. *The Godly Man in Stuart England; Anglicans, Puritans and the Two Tables, 1620–1670.* New Haven, CT: Yale University Press, 1976.

Miller, Howard. *The Revolutionary College, American Presbyterian Higher Education, 1707–1837.* New York: New York University Press, 1976.

Miller, Perry. *Errand into the Wilderness.* Cambridge: Belknap Press, a division of Harvard University Press, 1956; New York: Harper Torchbooks, Harper & Row, Publishers, 1964.

———. *The Puritans, A Sourcebook of Their Writings.* Edited by Perry Miller and Thomas Johnson. 2 vols. New York: Harper & Row, 1963.

Miller, Samuel. *Memoir of the Rev. John Rodgers, D.D.* Philadelphia: 1840.

Mueller, William. *Church and State in Luther and Calvin.* Nashville, TN: Broadman Press, 1954.

Nobles, Gregory. *Divisions Throughout the Whole, Politics and Society in Hampshire County, Massachusetts, 1740–1775.* Cambridge: Cambridge University Press, 1983.

Noll, Mark. *Christians in the American Revolution.* Washington, D.C.: Christian University Press, 1977.

Noll, Mark, Nathan Hatch, and George Marsden. *The Search for Christian America.* Westchester, IL: Crossway Books, 1983.

Pointer, Richard. *Protestant Pluralism and the New York Experience.* Bloomington, IN: Indiana University Press, 1988.

Robbins, Caroline. *The Eighteenth-Century Commonwealthman.* Cambridge: Harvard University Press, 1959.

Rossiter, Clinton. *The Political Thought of the American Revolution.* New York: Harcourt, Brace & World, Inc., 1963.

Sabine, George. *A History of Political Theory.* Third edition. New York: Holt, Rinehart, and Winston, 1961.

Schaff, Phillip. *Creeds of Christendom.* 3 vols. 1889; reprint, Grand Rapids, MI: Baker Book House, 1983.

Schlatter, Richard. *Richard Baxter and Puritan Politics.* New Brunswick, NJ: Rutgers University Press, 1957.

Seidensticker, Oswald. *The First Century of German Printing in America, 1728–1830.* 1893; reprint, New York: Kraus Reprint Corporation, 1966.

Skinner, Quentin. *The Foundations of Modern Political Thought.* Volume 2: The Age of Reformation. Cambridge: Cambridge University Press, 1978.

Sloan, Douglas. *The Scottish Enlightenment and the American College Ideal.* New York: Teachers College Press, 1971.

Smith, H. Shelton, Robert Handy, and Lefferts Loetscher. *American Christianity, An Historical Interpretation with Representative Documents.* 2 vols. New York: Charles Scribner's Sons, 1960.

Soderlund, Jean. *Quakers and Slavery, A Divided Spirit.* Princeton, NJ: Princeton University Press, 1985.

Spurlin, Paul. *Montesquieu in America, 1760–1801.* New York: Octagon Books, 1969.

Stone, Lawrence. *The Causes of the English Revolution, 1529–1642.* London: Routledge & Kegan Paul, 1972.

Stout, Harry. *The New England Soul.* New York: Oxford University Press, 1986.

Sweet, William W. *Religion in Colonial America.* New York: Charles Scribner's Sons, 1942.

Tanis, James. *Dutch Calvinistic Pietism in the Middle Colonies: A Study of the Life and Theology of Theodorus Jacobus Frelinghuysen.* The Hague, 1967.

Toon, Peter, ed. *Puritans, The Millennium and the Future of Israel: Puritan Eschatology 1600–1660.* London: James Clarke & Co., Ltd., 1970.

Trinterud, Leonard. *The Forming of an American Tradition, A Reexamination of Colonial Presbyterianism.* Philadelphia: Westminster Press, 1949.

Walker, Williston. *Creeds and Platforms of Congregationalism.* Philadelphia: Pilgrim Press, 1969.

Watts, Michael. *The Dissenters.* London: Clarendon Press, 1978.

Westerkamp, Marilyn. *Triumph of the Laity, Scots-Irish Piety and the Great Awakening, 1625–1760.* New York: Oxford University Press, 1988.

Wilson, John F. *Pulpit in Parliament.* Princeton, NJ: Princeton University Press, 1969.

b. Articles

Bainton, Roland. "Congregationalism: From the Just War to the Crusade in the Puritan Revolution." *Andover Newton Theological School Bulletin,* Southworth Lecture, 35 (April 1943): 1–20.

Beam, Christopher. "Millennialism and American Nationalism, 1740–1800." *Journal of Presbyterian History* 54 (1976): 182–99.

Beam, Jacob. "Dr. Robert Smith's Academy at Pequea, Pennsylvania." *Journal of the Presbyterian Historical Society* 8 (December 1915): 145–61.

Beardslee, John, III. "The Reformed Church and the American Revolution." In *Piety and Patriotism: Bicentennial Studies of the Reformed Church in America, 1776–1976.* Edited by James Van Hoeven. Grand Rapids, MI: Wm. B. Eerdmans, 1976; 17–33.

Bonomi, Patricia, " 'A Just Opposition': The Great Awakening as a Radical Model." In *The Origins of Anglo-American Radicalism.* Edited by Margaret Jacob and James Jacob. London: George Allen & Unwin, 1984; 243–56.

———. " 'Stewards of the Mysteries of God': Clerical Authority and the Great Awakening in the Middle Colonies." In *Professions and Professional Ideologies in America.* Edited by Gerald Geison. Chapel Hill, NC: University of North Carolina Press, 1983; 29–48.

Brauer, Jerald. "Regionalism and Religion in America." *Church History* 54 (September 1985): 366–78.

———. "Reflections on the Nature of English Puritanism." *Church History* 23 (June 1954): 99–108.

Briceland, Alan. "Daniel McCalla, 1748–1809: New Side Revolutionary and Jeffersonian." *Journal of Presbyterian History* 56 (Fall 1978): 252–69.

Brown, Thomas M. "The Image of the Beast: Anti-Papal Rhetoric in Colonial America." In *Conspiracy: the Fear of Subversion in American History.* Edited by Richard Curry and Thomas Brown. New York: Holt, Rinehart, and Winston, 1972.

Buchanan, John. "Puritan Philosophy of History from Restoration to Revolution." *Essex Institute Historical Collections* CIV (1968), 329–48.

Capp, Bernard. "Godly Rule and English Millennialism." *Past and Present* 52 (August 1971).

Clifton, Robin. "Fear of Popery." In *The Origins of the English Civil War.* Edited by Conrad Russell. London: Macmillan, 1973; 144–67.

Collinson, Patrick. "A Comment: Concerning the Name Puritan." *Journal of Ecclesiastical History* 31 (October 1980): 483–88.

Danner, Dan. "Christopher Goodman and the English Protestant Tradition of Civil Disobedience." *Sixteenth Century Journal* 8 (1977): 61–73.

————. "Resistance and the Ungodly Magistrate in the Sixteenth Century: the Marian Exiles." *Journal of the American Academy of Religion* 49 (September 1981): 471–81.

DeVries, George, Jr. "Church and State in New York, an Historical Account." *Reformed Journal* (November–December 1975); 18–21, 25–28.

Endy, Melvin, Jr. "Just War, Holy War, and Millennialism in Revolutionary America." *William and Mary Quarterly,* third ser., 42 (January 1985): 3–25.

Gamble, Richard. "The Christian and the Tyrant: Beza and Knox on Political Resistance Theory." *Westminster Theological Journal* 46 (Spring 1984): 125–39.

George, Timothy. "War and Peace in the Puritan Tradition." *Church History* 53 (December 1984): 492–503.

Gough, Robert. "The Myth of the 'Middle Colonies': An Analysis of Regionalism in Early America," *William and Mary Quarterly,* third ser., 107 (July 1983): 393–413.

Greenberg, Douglas. "The Middle Colonies in Recent American Historiography." *William and Mary Quarterly,* third ser., 36 (July 1979): 396–427.

Hatch, Nathan. "The Origins of Civil Millennialism in America: New England Clergymen, War with France, and the American Revolution." *William and Mary Quarterly,* third ser., 31 (July 1974): 407–30.

Hildebrandt, Esther. "The Magdeburg Bekenntnis as a Possible Link between German and English Resistance Theories in the Sixteenth Century." *Archiv für Reformationsgeschichte* 71 (1981): 227–52.

Hill, Christopher. "Recent Interpretations of the Civil War." In *Puritanism and Revolution.* 1958; reprint, New York: Schocken Books, 1967; 3–31.

Hudson, Winthrop. "Democratic Freedom and Religious Faith in the Reformed Tradition." *Church History* 15 (1946): 177–94.

Kennedy, Earl. "From Providence to Civil Religion: Some 'Dutch' Reformed Interpretations of America in the Revolutionary Era." *Reformed Review* 29 (September 1976): 111–23.

Kenney, Alice. "The Albany Dutch, Loyalists and Patriots." *New York History* 62 (October 1961): 331–50.

Kingdon, Robert. "The First Expression of Theodore Beza's Political Ideas." *Archiv für Reformationsgeschichte* 45 (1955): 88–99.

Kramer, Leonard. "Presbyterians Approach the American Revolution." *Journal of Presbyterian History* 31 (June–September 1953): 71–86, 167–80.

————. "Muskets in the Pulpit: 1776–83." *Journal of Presbyterian History* 31 and 32 (December 1953 and March 1954): 229–44 and 37–51, respectively.

Lodge, Martin. "The Crisis of the Churches in the Middle Colonies, 1720–1750." *Pennsylvania Magazine of History and Biography* 95 (April 1971): 195–220.

McAllister, James, Jr., "Francis Alison and John Witherspoon: Political Philosophers and Revolutionaries." *Journal of Presbyterian History* 54 (Spring 1976): 33–60.

Metzger, Charles. "Chaplains in the American Revolution." *Catholic Historical Review* 31 (April 1945): 31–79.

Murray, Nicholas. "A Memoir of the Rev. James Caldwell of Elizabethtown." *New Jersey Historical Society Proceedings*, ser. 1 (1848): 79–89.

Nobbs, D. "Phillip Nye on Church and State." *Cambridge Historical Journal* 5 (1935): 41–59.

Noll, Mark. "Observations on the Reconciliation of Politics and Religion in the Revolutionary New Jersey: the Case Jacob Green." *Journal of Presbyterian History* 54 (Summer 1976): 217–37.

Nuttall, Geoffrey. "The First Non-Conformists." In *From Uniformity to Unity, 1662–1692*. Edited by Geoffrey Nuttall and Owen Chadwick. London, 1962.

Rightmyer, Nelson. "Churches Under Enemy Occupation, Philadelphia, 1777–8." *Church History* 14 (1945): 33–60.

Riley, Jobie. "The Rhetoric of the German-Speaking Pulpit in Eighteenth-Century Pennsylvania," *Journal of the Lancaster County Historical Society*. Trinity, 1977.

Robbins, Caroline. " 'When It Is That Colonies May Turn Independent': An Analysis of the Environment and Politics of Francis Hutcheson (1694–1746)." *William and Mary Quarterly*, third ser., 11 (April 1954): 214–51.

Savelle, Max. "Nationalism and Other Loyalties in the American Revolution." *American Historical Review* 67 (July 1962), 901–23.

Smylie, James. "Presbyterian Clergy and Problems of 'Dominion' in the Revolutionary Generation." *Journal of Presbyterian History* 48 (Fall 1970): 161–75.

Solt, Leo. "Revolutionary Calvinist Parties in England under Elizabeth I and Charles I." *Church History* 27 (1958): 234–39.

Spalding, James. "Loyalist as Royalist, Patriot as Puritan: The American Revolution as a Repetition of the English Civil Wars." *Church History* 45 (1976): 329–40.

————. "Sermons before Parliament (1640–49) as a Public Puritan Diary." *Church History* 36 (1967): 24–35.

Stark, Rodney, and Roger Finke. "American Religion in 1776: A Statistical Portrait." *Sociological Analysis* 49 (Spring 1988): 39–51.

Stout, Harry. "The Puritans and Edwards." In *Jonathan Edwards and the American Experience*. Edited by Nathan Hatch and Harry Stout. New York: Oxford University Press, 1988; 142–59.

————. "Religion, Communications, and the Ideological Origins of the American Revolution." *William and Mary Quarterly*, third ser., 34 (October 1977): 519–41.

Tyacke, Nicholas. "Puritanism, Arminianism, and Counter Revolution." In *Origins of the English Civil War*. Edited by Conrad Russell. New York: Macmillan, 1973; 119–43.

Van Tyne, Claude. "Influences of the Clergy, and of Religious and Sectarian Forces, on the American Revolution." *American Historical Review* 19 (October 1913): 44–64.

Wedgewood, C. V. "The Trial of Charles I." In *The English Civil War and After, 1642–1658*. Edited by R. H. Parry. Berkeley: University of California Press, 1970; 41–58.

Weinstein, Minne. "Stephen Marshall and the Dilemma of the Political Puritan." *Journal of Presbyterian History* 46 (1968): 1–25.

Wollman, David. "The Biblical Justification for Resistance to Authority in Ponet's and Goodman's Polemics." *Sixteenth Century Journal* 13 (1982): 29–41.

c. Dissertations

Balmer, Randall. "Dutch Religion in an English World: Political Upheaval and Ethnic Conflict in the Middle Colonies." Ph.D. diss., Princeton University, 1985.

Dawson, J.E.A. "The Early Career of Christopher Goodman and His Place in the Development of English Protestant Thought." Ph.D. diss., University of Durham, 1978.

Gordon, Ann. "The College of Philadelphia, 1749–1779: Impact of an Institution." Ph.D. diss., University of Wisconsin, 1975.

Johnson, Lee. "An Examination of the Role of John Gano in the Development of Baptist Life in North America, 1750–1804." Ph.D. diss., Southwestern Baptist Theological Seminary, 1986.

Jungen, Christoph. "Calvin and the Origin of Political Resistance Theory in the Calvinist Tradition." Th.M. thesis, Westminster Theological Seminary, 1980.

Klunder, Jack. "The Application of Holy Things: A Study of the Covenant Preaching in the Eighteenth Century Dutch Colonial Church." Ph.D. diss., Westminster Theological Seminary, 1985.

Kramer, Leonard. "The Political Ethics of the American Presbyterian Clergy in the Eighteenth Century." Ph.D. diss., Yale University, 1942.

Kraus, Joe. "Book Collections of Five Colonial College Libraries: A Subject Analysis." Ph.D. diss., University of Illinois, Urbana, 1960.

Luidens, John. "The Americanization of the Dutch Reformed Church." Ph.D. diss., University of Oklahoma, 1969.

Marston, Jerrilyn. "King and Congress: the Transfer of Political Legitimacy from the King to the Continental Congress, 1774–1776." Ph.D. diss., Boston University, 1975.

Smoot, John. "Presbyterianism in Revolutionary Pennsylvania: Constitutionalism and Freedom." Ph.D. diss., St. Mary's Seminary and University, 1982.

Wingo, Barbara. "Politics, Society, and Religion: The Presbyterian Clergy of Pennsylvania, New Jersey, and New York, and the Formation of the Nation, 1775–1808." Ph.D. diss., Tulane University, 1976.

Index